RETURN *TO* SUNDAY DINNER

Revised and Expanded

THE SIMPLE DELIGHT *of* FAMILY, FRIENDS, *and* FOOD

RUSSELL CRONKHITE

THOMAS NELSON
Since 1798

NASHVILLE   DALLAS   MEXICO CITY   RIO DE JANEIRO

Published in Nashville, Tennessee, by Thomas Nelson. Thomas Nelson is a registered trademark of Thomas Nelson, Inc.

Photographs by Koechel Peterson and Associates, Inc., Minneapolis, Minnesota

Photographs on pages 7, 20, 36, 65, 67, 99, 109, 141, 154, 158, 181, 187, 190, 201, 203, 206, 267 taken by Ron Manville and styled by Teresa Blackburn

Photographs on pages 71, 121, 135 from fotolia.com

Thomas Nelson, Inc., titles may be purchased in bulk for educational, business, fund-raising, or sales promotional use. For information, please e-mail SpecialMarkets@ ThomasNelson.com.

Page design by Walter Petrie

Library of Congress Cataloging-in-Publication Data

Cronkhite, Russell.
  Return to Sunday dinner : the simple delight of family, friends, and food / Russell Cronkhite. — Revised & updated.
    pages cm
  ISBN 978-1-4016-0480-6 (hardback)
  1. Dinners and dining. I. Title.
  TX737.C76 2012
  641.5'4—dc23   2012019229

Printed in the United States of America

12 13 14 15 16 QGF 6 5 4 3 2 1

Contents

Welcome to Our Table

Remember Sunday dinner? Just hearing the words can take you back—perhaps to a well-loved dining room in your grandparents' house, where a stately oak table is laid with lace and hand-painted china. The table overflows with its Sunday bounty . . . bowls of steaming, garden-fresh vegetables, crocks of sweet butter and homemade jam, and the succulent Sunday roast, juicy and brown. Incomparable aromas fill the house, laden with the promise of freshly baked, light-as-a-feather biscuits or warm-from-the-oven peach cobbler.

Perhaps your memories of Sunday dinner are something else entirely. I found this to be the case when I brought up the subject at a recent gathering of friends. Everyone, it seemed, had a favorite Sunday-dinner memory to relate—and everyone was fiercely committed to his or her memory. The delightful sharing soon turned into a debate over whose mother made the best fried chicken, whether or not pot roast should be cooked with turnips, what kind of cheese goes best with macaroni, and whether mashed potatoes should have lumps!

Why did we get so worked up? I think it's because the subject of Sunday dinner taps into something deep within us. It's about family and faith and meaning and memories—and something even deeper. Can you feel it? Whether your passions are equal to my friends'—or even if Sunday dinner isn't part of your personal past at all—surely you know the tug of longing for a special day, a weekly refuge of love and laughter, peace and plenty, comfort and tradition.

Sunday dinner was once an American institution, a strong, familiar thread running deeply through our national fabric. I believe it can be that way again. A return to Sunday dinner can help bring us back to a time of craftsmanship, honor, values, and care. It can show us once again that time spent with those we love—enjoying games, listening to tales, sharing our dreams and disappointments, and simply enjoying time together—far outweighs the amusements of the hectic, impersonal world that presses in all around us.

And now is the time to build those traditions anew. The book you hold in your hands is a call to launch your own Sunday dinner heritage, creating fresh and indelible memories for generations to come.

It's a call to rediscover Sunday dinner in your own life.

In a sense, Sunday dinner is a gift we can give to one another and pass on to our children and our children's children. It's a much-needed respite of rest, celebration, and inspiration.

In years gone by, whether in small towns, on the farm, or in great cities, most Americans took Sunday off. And rested. Shops and markets closed their doors. Twenty-four-hour groceries, shopping malls, and so-called convenience stores belonged to the unimaginable future. Life slowed for one day a week: a day for worship and quiet reflection, a day for relaxation and restoration, a day for family, a day apart from the everyday bustle.

Even in past centuries, setting apart a weekly day of rest required a certain discipline. Families worked hard to plan and prepare for the day when work would be laid aside. And unfortunately, religious curmudgeons sometimes made this special day feel like a day of repression, as though "day of rest" meant "day of no fun." But surely this was a corruption of the original intention—a misuse of the gift of Sunday rest.

In my experience, at least, such joyless legalism was never the norm for Sunday dinner. Sunday was different, yes, but different in a way that made things better for everyone. It was a day of rest, to be sure, but it was also a true day of celebration—a time to delight in the company of loved ones, to review and rebuild the unwritten customs of our past, and to enjoy together a bounty of wholesome foods. This includes the scrumptious traditional meals our parents, grandparents, and great-grandparents brought to this country, for food—along with language, religion, and art—is one of the essential pillars of any culture.

Throughout history, special meals have come to symbolize special times, and such meals mark our family lives as well: birthday dinners, reunion picnics, weddings, anniversaries. When other details of past events fade, the flavors of the food we shared together linger in the memory. And year after year, as holidays approach, we relish with anticipation the savory tastes and aromas we've come to associate with those annual festivities.

The Sunday table, too, has always been a center for family celebrations. Restful Sundays provide us with unhurried hours for enjoying our shared lives—exploring our heritage, remembering the sacrifices of those who made our lives possible, and giving thanks for God's kindness and blessings.

But the Sunday dinner offers even more than true rest and joyful celebration. It also provides something often overlooked in this casual age: the gift of encouragement and inspiration. It helps us remember that there is indeed something beyond and above our commonplace world.

When architects created the great cathedrals of Europe, they sought to inspire—and they succeeded. The grand arches draw our eyes up and away from everyday life to contemplate the very heights of heaven. They mark a space and a time that is special and set apart.

The Sunday table has the ability to lift us up as well, to remind us that there is more to life than just daily bread. That's why Sunday dinner has always been a time to break out our very best—to set our finest table, elegant or cheerful with beautiful linens and dishes, bright with flowers, and bountiful with platters of our favorite foods.

And what an inspiring transformation Sunday can bring! The everyday table, rushed with kids, piled with homework, where we read the morning paper, is transformed and set apart. A tablecloth covers the ordinary wood. The china may not be showpiece quality, but it gleams with meaning and memories. The centerpiece flowers give humble testimony to the beauty of creation. We dress in our nicest clothes, put on our company manners. And the meal itself—carefully planned, lovingly prepared, and gratefully shared—provides a vivid and delicious and, yes, inspirational picture of what life can be.

I was fortunate to enjoy such Sunday celebrations with my family when I was growing up. My mother, my two sisters, my brother, and I loved to spend Sunday afternoons at our grandparents' home. Cousins, aunts, and uncles gathered there as well. Birthdays and special holidays such as Memorial Day, Easter, and Mother's Day became much-anticipated and long-remembered reunions.

My grandmother did most of the cooking, although we all pitched in to keep her Sunday workload light. Grandma was a pioneer, raised in the heart of Texas. Her mother's family was of sturdy Scots-Irish descent. Her father and uncle had walked the old war trails from the Eastern Cherokee Nation in Georgia to Texas and the Oklahoma territories. And it was in Oklahoma that Grandma met Grandpa at his tenth birthday party. His family had traveled there from Virginia, and the party took place as both families prepared their covered wagons for the long journey farther west. Their families would be among the last of those that traveled the old trails toward California and Oregon. And although the two families took different routes west, my grandparents remembered each other. Remarkably, they found each other on the West Coast and eventually married. Grandpa went to work for the railroad, and their five children were born up and down the Union Pacific line, from Seattle to Los Angeles.

My grandparents were never rich. Like many Depression-era families, they learned to make do with what they had. They ate simple, well-balanced meals, freshly prepared with wholesome but inexpensive ingredients. But those meals must have had some merit: Both of my grandparents lived to nearly ninety years of age.

Our table was mostly Southern in influence: black-eyed peas and corn bread for good luck on New Year's Day, baked ham for Easter. But we also enjoyed many other American standards—New England boiled dinner, Yankee pot roast, and home-baked beans—found in classic volumes on American cookery by Mary Randolph, Mrs. T. J. Crowen, and Fannie Farmer.

For me, growing up with little never meant having less.

The Sunday meal was always memorable.

When my wife and I began a family of our own twenty-five years ago, we wanted to build the same kinds of Sunday memories. So Sunday became our family day, the day we would spend together. First, we would attend church as a family. Then later, if one child had a soccer game, for instance, we'd all go to the game. If such activities conflicted with our normal dinnertime, we'd bring a snack and plan for a family meal later in the day. Or we'd eat a light breakfast so our midday dinner could be enjoyed early.

To the best of our ability, we guarded our Sundays together—not out of some legalistic obsession or obligation, but simply because we wanted a day away from the worries of the world and the often frantic pace of everyday life. We wanted to carve out a day of retreat, a day of rest, one day a week to just enjoy each other.

On many Sundays, we would try to plan something special for the day—an activity that was both leisurely and family oriented. Sometimes we'd set off to explore a museum. Other times we'd head for the countryside. And like so many families, we enjoyed going out for an occasional Sunday brunch—a nice break from the labors of our own kitchen.

Most Sundays, however, we cooked our Sunday dinner. Cooking was part of the fun—something we enjoyed doing together—as was sitting down to real Sunday dinner with friends and family. The Sunday dinner table became the place where we could share thoughts as well as food and discuss the questions of the day, often with guests. It was the place where our children learned good manners, how to carry on meaningful conversations, to be gracious hosts—setting an inviting table and clearing as guests enjoyed after-dinner discussion—and to help in the kitchen, which equipped them with useful life skills.

Sunday by Sunday, we added treasured pages to the albums of our memories. And because Sunday dinner has always been special to us, I suppose it's no surprise that it even became a part of my professional life.

For more than thirty-five years, I have been privileged to make a living as a professional chef. I worked in some of the finest establishments in this country. But by far the most memorable segment of my career was my nearly twelve years as executive chef of Blair House, the presidential guest house, located across Pennsylvania Avenue from the White House.

Since 1942, Blair House has catered to our nation's most important guests. During my tour of duty there, I had the honor of serving three presidents, as well as nearly every major world leader of that era—from Queen Elizabeth II and Prince Philip to Nelson Mandela, Mother Teresa, Boris Yeltsin, Margaret Thatcher, Prime Minister Benazir Bhutto of Pakistan, President Vaclav Havel of the Czech Republic, the emperor and empress of Japan, President François Mitterrand of France, and President Jiang Zemin of China.

While many of the meals we served during that time were exquisite formal banquets, many were the well-loved, familiar kinds of meals that reflect the bounty of our nation—the simple yet wonderful tastes that make up what we know as regional American foods.

And through those years, when I was asked about the traditional dishes we prepared and the hospitality Blair House offered, I had a ready reply:

"Just think of Sunday dinner."

It is my hope that this book will help you think of Sunday dinner in your own life. It is a full-hearted celebration of our American culture—our deep religious heritage, our unique regional cuisine, and our time-honored traditions of hospitality, welcome, and ease.

But *Return to Sunday Dinner* is meant to be more than a beautiful book filled with tempting recipes. I hope it will inspire you to create your own special Sunday dinners for family and friends—and to do so with aplomb and ease.

Sunday dinner is meant to be special, after all—a true celebration—but it is also the highlight of a day of rest. Recognizing this, I chose and developed the recipes in this volume with an eye toward simple preparation. There is no meal in this book that cannot be created by a cook (or cooks) of moderate skill, from ingredients that are readily available in your local grocery.

Sunday dinner, I believe, can be both a touchstone to our past and a foundation on which to build memories. Whether or not Sunday dinner is part of your personal past, this weekly time of rest, celebration, and inspiration can be part of your life right now. This book is all the invitation you need.

It's Sunday, and dinner's ready.

Chapter 1

OUR SUNDAY BEST

BUTTER-STEAMED BROCCOLI

SUNDAY'S BEST ROAST
BEEF *with* PAN GRAVY

SOUR CREAM MASHED POTATOES

SESAME CLOVERLEAF ROLLS

GLAZED BABY CARROTS

BITTERSWEET CHOCOLATE
BUTTERMILK CAKE

Remember that phrase "Sunday best"? When I was a child, I heard it at least once a week. Sunday was when we wore our nicest clothes and shoes, all pressed and mended and shined, and tried to remember our company manners. We set the table with our most beautiful linens and china, and feasted on the most delectable foods we could afford. It wasn't a way of showing off, but a way of showing respect.

In the American culinary tradition, the Sunday roast represents that ideal. When meat was a luxury, when good-quality tender meat was expensive and hard to find, we saved the choicest cut of beef for the Sunday dinner table.

By definition, a roasted piece of meat is succulent, tender, and juicy, with a caramelized seasoned crust on the outside and a pink juicy middle. Until the late nineteenth century, large cuts of meat were roasted on a spit over hot coals or in an open-hearth kitchen, turned continually, and then basted with the drippings caught in a pan below the spit. Great care was needed to cook the meat properly and safely. The modern oven changed all that, but a tender, well-cooked roast is still a culinary triumph.

My own childhood memories often carry me back to my grandmother's table on roast-beef Sundays. Grandma didn't dish food onto plates in the kitchen like a diner. Everything came to the table in steaming bowls—mashed potatoes, hand-whipped and creamy; bright green broccoli dripping with golden butter; hot, soft rolls fresh from the oven and covered with a napkin—all set before us in silence. Last came the roast, crusty, rare, and dripping with juice, arranged on Grandma's best platter with thin slices laid around the edges and the remainder standing ready to be carved for seconds.

After dinner, when the table had been cleared, a tall, moist chocolate cake would be uncovered and cut with a silver cake service. Each plated slice was passed from hand to hand round the table, with all the children hoping the biggest piece would stop with them. Then came cups of good strong coffee for the adults and more cold milk for the kids (which was always poured from a pitcher).

This was Sunday dinner as I remember it, Sunday as it was meant to be—and still can be. Careful handiwork, loving preparation, mouthwatering food, and family and guests gathered around a beautifully set table. It's all quite simply the best: our Sunday best.

BUTTER-STEAMED BROCCOLI

Broccoli is such a wonderful, good-for-you vegetable. When grocery shopping, look for a head of broccoli with a tight, firm flower. Frozen florets are an excellent alternative to fresh. Steaming broccoli will reveal its vibrant color, as well as help it to retain more nutrients. The touch of butter will bring out its full flavor without adding any significant fat or calories.

2 pounds fresh or thawed frozen broccoli

2 tablespoons butter

Pinch of salt

First, if using fresh broccoli, trim 3 to 4 inches of the heavy stalk from the bottom of each broccoli flower with a sharp paring knife; then split each stalk lengthwise through its stem into 3 or 4 pieces. Avoid cutting through the small tender buds when possible; keeping the florets whole and the large stems thin will help the broccoli cook evenly.

Second, place the broccoli in a shallow saucepan—make sure it is wide enough that there are no more than two layers of broccoli. Pour in just enough water to cover the bottom of the pan by 1/2 inch. Add the butter and pinch of salt.

Third, bring the water to a full boil over medium-high heat. Place a tight-fitting lid over the pan and steam the broccoli until just tender, 5 to 6 minutes.

Fourth, drain the liquid from the saucepan and arrange the steamed broccoli in a serving bowl. Garnish, if desired, with a pat of butter; serve immediately.

SUNDAY'S BEST ROAST BEEF
with PAN GRAVY

8 Servings

A great Sunday roast comes in many forms: standing rib, eye of the top round, bottom round, or—my favorite—a rump roast. (The rump is the tender tip of the round.) My mother always picked a larger-than-needed roast; then we'd enjoy great roast beef sandwiches and often a hearty stew from the leftover meat.

ROAST BEEF

I (4- to 5-pound) boneless rump roast

I tablespoon Worcestershire sauce

I teaspoon granulated garlic

I teaspoon onion powder

1/2 teaspoon paprika

2 teaspoons coarse-ground black pepper

2 teaspoons coarse salt

PAN GRAVY

3 tablespoons all-purpose flour

2 cups beef broth

Salt and pepper to taste

Oven temperature 450°F.

Prepare the roast: First, blot any excess moisture from the roast using paper towels. Rub the Worcestershire sauce over the entire roast; allow the roast to sit for a few minutes, turning it several times so that the meat can absorb the Worcestershire.

Second, combine the granulated garlic, onion powder, paprika, and coarse-ground pepper in a small bowl; sprinkle the seasoning mixture evenly over the roast, pressing it into the fat and meat just enough to stick. Allow the seasoned roast to stand at room temperature for 20 to 30 minutes before roasting.

Third, rub the roast with the coarse salt and place it fat side up in a shallow roasting pan. Place the roast on the bottom rack of the oven. Roast for 15 minutes and then lower the oven temperature to 325°F. Continue to cook until the internal temperature reaches 5 to 10 degrees below the desired serving temperature, about 2 hours. (Note: Allow about 20 minutes per pound

for medium-rare.) When the roast is done, carefully remove the pan from the oven and transfer the roast to a clean cutting board. Allow the roast to stand for 20 minutes before slicing.

Make the gravy: Use a spoon to skim all the fat from the liquid that remains in the roasting pan. Reserve about 4 tablespoons of fat in a small mixing bowl and cool until it is just barely warm, 4 to 5 minutes. Whisk the flour into the fat to form a roux. (Note: For low-fat gravy, you may replace the fat with 1/4 cup of water.) Scrape the drippings from the bottom of the pan, add in the beef broth, and stir over medium heat until the broth begins to simmer. Whisk in the roux and bring to a boil. Simmer for 4 to 5 minutes. Add a little water, a tablespoon at a time, as needed to achieve the desired consistency. Season to taste with salt and pepper.

Present the roast: Use a sharp carving knife to cut thin slices against the grain. Arrange the slices on a decorative platter and pour the irresistible juices left on the cutting board over the meat. Pass the gravy alongside in a gravy boat.

SOUR CREAM MASHED POTATOES

8 Servings ▪ ▪ ▪ ▪ ▪ ▪ ▪ ▪ ▪ ▪ ▪ ▪ ▪ ▪ ▪ ▪ ▪ ▪ ▪

The key to truly great mashed potatoes is starting with great potatoes. In my opinion, the very best are White Rose or Yukon Gold. I find that russets are better for baking and that starchy potatoes, such as red-skins, are better for roasting.

8 medium Yukon Gold potatoes

1/2 cup (1 stick) butter

2/3 cup whole milk

1 cup sour cream

1 tablespoon fresh snipped chives

Salt to taste

First, peel and quarter the potatoes. Cut each quarter in half and place in a large pot filled with enough cool salted water to cover them completely. Bring to a boil, reduce the heat to a robust simmer (not a rolling boil) and let the potatoes cook undisturbed until they are just beginning to fall apart, 20 to 25 minutes.

Second, drain off the water and return the pot to the stove. Let the potatoes cook for a minute, shaking the pot to evaporate the excess moisture. Add in the butter and continue to shake the pot until the butter melts completely and coats all of the potatoes (this will keep the potatoes from becoming sticky when they are mashed). Pour in the milk and heat until it begins to boil.

Third, remove the potatoes from the heat. Use a potato masher or stiff wire whip to thoroughly mash the potatoes in an up-and-down motion. Add in the sour cream and whip just until they are smooth. (Note: Do not whip too hard or for too long or the potatoes will be sticky, not fluffy.)

Fourth, fold in the chives and season to taste with salt. Garnish, if desired, with snipped chives.

SESAME CLOVERLEAF ROLLS

With their golden crusts and light, airy centers, cloverleaf rolls are always a favorite—and they are so easy to make. I like them plain as well as sprinkled with sesame seeds.

1 package (1 ½ teaspoons) active dry yeast

¼ cup warm water, about 110°F

1 cup whole milk

2 tablespoons granulated sugar

½ cup (1 stick) butter

2 large eggs, room temperature

1 large egg yolk, room temperature

3 ½ cups all-purpose flour, divided

1 teaspoon salt

1 large egg white, room temperature, well beaten

2 tablespoons sesame seeds

Oven temperature 400°F.

First, sprinkle the yeast over the water and let stand for 1 minute. Stir until the yeast is dissolved.

Second, scald the milk with the sugar by heating it in a small saucepan to the point of boiling. Remove it from the heat and swirl in the butter until it melts completely. Cool in the pan until lukewarm.

Third, lightly beat the 2 eggs and the egg yolk together; combine with the dissolved yeast and the lukewarm milk. Then stir in 2 cups of the flour. Continue stirring until the batter is smooth and elastic, about 120 strokes. Scrape down the sides of the bowl with a rubber spatula. Cover the bowl with a clean tea towel and place in a draft-free place until the dough is bubbly and has doubled in volume, about 1 hour.

Fourth, whisk the salt into the remaining 1^1/$_2$ cups of flour. Use an electric mixer fitted with a dough hook to slowly incorporate the flour mixture into the bubbly dough on low speed. Scrape down the sides of the bowl with a rubber spatula. Increase the mixer speed to medium and add in a little extra flour as necessary, a tablespoon at a time, until the dough begins to pull away from the sides of the bowl. Reduce the mixer speed to low and knead for 5 minutes; the dough should attain a smooth, soft, silky texture. Dust the dough with a little flour to keep it from sticking to your hands and form it into a ball. Place in a lightly oiled bowl and cover with plastic wrap. Refrigerate for at least 30 minutes and up to 4 hours.

Fifth, divide the dough into 6 equal pieces and roll the pieces between your hands into 12-inch ropes. Divide each rope into 12 equal pieces and roll the pieces into little balls. Place 3 balls into each of 24 lightly greased muffin tins. Use a pastry brush to glaze the tops of the rolls with the beaten egg white, and then sprinkle with the sesame seeds. Cover the rolls with a clean tea towel, set in a draft-free place and let them rise until doubled in size, about 1 hour.

Sixth, bake for 12 to 15 minutes. Brush the tops with melted butter while the rolls are still hot.

GLAZED BABY CARROTS

8 Servings

Tiny carrots are sweet all by themselves. The addition of butter, honey, and orange juice brings out their naturally sweet flavor even more, making the simple sublime.

4 cups peeled baby carrots

¹/₄ cup (¹/₂ stick) butter

¹/₄ cup honey

I cup freshly squeezed orange juice

First, place the carrots into a skillet of boiling salted water and simmer until they are tender on the outside and still crunchy in the middle (al dente), 4 to 6 minutes. Drain off the water.

Second, add the butter to the drained carrots and continue cooking over medium heat just long enough to melt the butter. Toss the carrots in the melted butter, then add in the honey and orange juice; blend together until the liquid begins bubbling. Simmer for 6 to 8 minutes, tossing the carrots from time to time, until the liquid is reduced to a glistening glaze.

To serve: Spoon the carrots into a warm dish and pour the glaze over top.

BITTERSWEET CHOCOLATE BUTTERMILK CAKE

12 Servings

Without a doubt, this chocolate cake is Sunday dinner dessert at its best! Nothing could be more truly American than moist, dense layers of cake and oh-so-satisfying chocolate-fudge frosting.

CHOCOLATE CAKE

2 1/4 cups cake flour

2 teaspoons baking soda

1/2 teaspoon salt

4 ounces bittersweet chocolate

2 ounces unsweetened chocolate

1 cup vegetable shortening

2 cups granulated sugar

2 teaspoons pure vanilla extract

4 large eggs, room temperature

1 cup buttermilk

FROSTING

4 ounces bittersweet chocolate

4 ounces unsweetened chocolate

1 1/2 cups (3 sticks) unsalted butter, chilled

1/4 cup light corn syrup

2 cups heavy cream

1 1/2 cups granulated sugar

2 teaspoons pure vanilla extract

Oven temperature 350°F.

Make the cake layers: First, grease and lightly flour two 9-inch round cake pans with 2-inch sides. Sift together the cake flour, baking soda, and salt in a medium bowl. Set aside.

Second, melt the bittersweet and unsweetened chocolate in a small dish in the microwave for 90 seconds or over medium heat in a small pan on the stove. Stir until smooth, then cool to room temperature.

Third, combine the shortening and sugar in the bowl of a mixer fitted with a paddle; cream together on medium-high speed until light and fluffy for 6 to 8 minutes. Turn the mixer off and scrape down the sides of the bowl with a rubber spatula, then add in the vanilla and the melted, cooled chocolate. Mix at medium-low speed until the chocolate is completely incorporated. Add in the eggs one at a time, mixing well after each addition.

Fourth, turn the mixer speed down to low. Add in the sifted dry ingredients in 3 batches alternately with the buttermilk, beating thoroughly after each addition to fully incorporate all of the ingredients. Do not overmix.

Fifth, divide the batter evenly between the prepared pans. Place the pans on the middle oven rack and bake for 30 minutes. The cakes are done when they begin to pull away from the edges of the pan and spring back when pressed gently in the center.

Sixth, allow the layers to cool in the pans for 10 minutes on wire racks before carefully running a thin sharp knife around the inside edge of each pan to loosen. Turn the cake layers out onto a cooling rack.

Prepare the frosting: First, chop the bittersweet and unsweetened chocolate into tiny pieces and slice the cold butter into 1-inch pats. Combine the butter and chocolate in the bowl of a food processor fitted with a steel blade.

Second, combine the corn syrup, cream, sugar, and vanilla in a medium saucepan. Stir constantly over medium-high heat until the sugar fully dissolves and the mixture comes to a boil. Continue cooking for 2 more minutes, stirring to keep the syrupy mixture from boiling over; then remove from heat and swirl gently until the bubbling subsides.

Third, immediately pour the hot cream mixture over the chocolate and butter. Quickly secure the processor lid and blend until the chocolate and

butter are blended thoroughly with the cream, about 1 minute. (Note: If you don't have a food processor, place the chocolate and butter in a mixing bowl, pour in the scalded cream mixture and whisk vigorously for 3 to 4 minutes.)

Fourth, pour the frosting into a glass dish and press a sheet of plastic wrap directly onto the surface. Let the frosting rest at room temperature for approximately 2 hours (do not refrigerate), until thick enough to hold soft peaks.

Assemble the cake: Place 1 layer of the cake on a cake stand. Use an icing spatula or table knife to spread about 1/3 of the frosting evenly on the cake. Place the second layer over the first and cover the top and sides with the remaining frosting. Cover the cake with a dome or bowl and keep at room temperature for up to one day.

Easy Time-Saving and Do-Ahead Tips

SATURDAY:

- Bake the cake layers, cool, and wrap tightly with plastic wrap. Prepare the cake frosting and allow to cool at room temperature; assemble the cake.

- Trim and portion the broccoli, transfer to a well-sealed container and refrigerate.

SUNDAY MORNING:

- Prepare the dough for the rolls and refrigerate.

- Peel and cut the potatoes; place in a pot and cover with cold water.

- Remove the roast from the refrigerator and bring to room temperature before seasoning.

- An hour and a half before dinner: Shape the rolls and let them rise.

Chapter 2

FROM HEARTH and HOME

FAMILY FAVORITE MEATLOAF
with BROWN SUGAR GLAZE

WHITE CHEDDAR POTATO BAKE

STONE-GROUND CORN MUFFINS

GARDEN PEA *and* CABBAGE SALAD

HONEY-HAZELNUT ACORN SQUASH

FARMHOUSE RHUBARB LATTICE PIE

Each of us has a vision of what a perfect Sunday afternoon should be. We gather together with family and friends around the amber glow of an inviting hearth, wrapping ourselves in the toasty warmth of the coals and in the comfort of our loved ones. We rejoice in familiar sights and sounds—children running and laughing, and bustling sounds from the kitchen And floating through it all are the warm, enticing aromas of an unforgettable Sunday dinner—a warm, inviting meal bright with family favorites.

Home, in other words, is where your heart is.

Perhaps it is the ambience of the hearth that sparks such reflections: The soft flames dancing bright from a crackling fire. The deep hues of brick or stone, held tight for the ages with mortar. Family pictures and treasured mementos lined up on a hand-carved mantle and the soothing warmth of the hearth itself.

The hearth was once the center of every home; it was the source of heat, the place where meals were cooked. While most of us now have furnaces and kitchens, people still gravitate toward the dancing warmth of a fireside. Here is a place for quiet contemplation, a place to cozy up with a favorite quilt, to enjoy a book or read the Sunday paper or simply sit and talk. Even in homes without fireplaces, Americans still gather around the hearth of friendship and family to cherish the many blessings we share.

The flavors of hearth and home are found throughout our land; they are as varied as our heritage. Few capture those flavors quite so well, though, as the foods rooted in Indiana and in the Ohio River Valley, where the influences of the Shaker communities have been passed down for us to enjoy.

Shaker communities once flourished from Maine to Kentucky. These set-apart religious communities were committed to excellence in all that they set out to do—from their elegantly simple handmade furniture and implements to their renowned apple cider. The Shakers were farmers, and theirs was a world rich with the simple tastes of homemade goodness: bread-and-butter pickles, green-tomato relish, apple butter, abundant fruit pies, maple syrup, and unadorned wholesome foods. Who doesn't love the roasted flavor of a moist and meaty meatloaf, creamy cheddar potatoes, baked squash, and corn muffins longing to be spread with butter, honey, or homemade jam? Such simple and satisfying recipes are the ones our taste buds and our hearts most long for, all flavored with the memories of hearth and home—Sunday dinner as it was meant to be.

FAMILY FAVORITE MEATLOAF
with BROWN SUGAR GLAZE

8 Servings

I like meatloaf that tastes meaty—seasoned carefully to enhance the beefy flavor but not overpower—and with a tasty and tangy glaze. Ground beef often comes from the butcher either as ground chuck, ground round, or ground sirloin; more and more it is sold not by cut but by fat ratio. For best results use fresh ground round or chuck between $85/15$ and $80/20$. Keep all of the ingredients cold while mixing together.

MEATLOAF

2/3 cup finely diced carrots

2/3 cup finely diced onion

1/3 cup finely diced bell pepper

1 tablespoon butter

4 slices white bread, trimmed and cubed

1/2 cup cold milk

2 pounds ground beef

2 teaspoons salt

1/2 teaspoon ground black pepper

1/2 teaspoon dried marjoram leaves

2 large eggs

3 tablespoons tomato ketchup

2 teaspoons Worcestershire sauce

GLAZE

1/2 cup tomato ketchup

2 tablespoons dark brown sugar

2 tablespoons cider vinegar

1/4 teaspoon Worcestershire sauce

Oven temperature 350°F.

Prepare the meatloaf: First, sauté the diced carrots, onion, and bell pepper in the butter for 1 minute. Cover the pan with a lid, turn off the heat and sweat the vegetables for 2 minutes. Uncover, cool to room temperature, and refrigerate. Place the bread cubes into a small mixing bowl and soak the bread cubes in the milk.

Second, place the cold ground beef into a non-corrosive mixing bowl. Mix in the salt, pepper, and marjoram. Add the eggs and mix into the seasoned beef until thoroughly combined. For best results, use your hands to gently mix in the ingredients. Thoroughly mix in the soaked bread, followed by the sautéed vegetables. Finally, mix in the ketchup and Worcestershire sauce. Cover and refrigerate for at least one hour.

Third, remove the meatloaf mixture from the refrigerator. Evenly shape the mixture into a loaf approximately 5 x 9 inches and place the loaf into a large shallow ceramic baking dish. Bake for 50 minutes.

To make the glaze: Whisk together the remaining ketchup, brown sugar, vinegar, and Worcestershire in a small bowl and set aside.

Finally, brush the top and sides of the meatloaf with the glaze and bake for an additional 10 minutes or until the internal temperature reaches 160°F. Let the meatloaf rest for 10 minutes before serving.

WHITE CHEDDAR POTATO BAKE

Using sharp cheddar from Oregon or aged cheddar from Vermont makes these potatoes particularly flavorful. This dish is also a great way to use up any leftover mashed potatoes.

8 medium white potatoes

1/2 cup (1 stick) butter

1/2 cup whole milk

1 large egg

Salt and pepper to taste

2 cups grated cheddar cheese

Oven temperature 350°F.

First, peel the potatoes and quarter them. Cut each quarter in half and place the potatoes in a large pot filled with enough cool salted water to cover them completely. Bring to a boil, reduce the heat to a robust simmer (not a rolling boil) and let the potatoes cook undisturbed until they are just beginning to fall apart, 20 to 25 minutes. Drain the water from the potatoes.

Second, return the pot to the stove and let the potatoes cook for 1 minute, shaking the pan to evaporate the excess moisture. Add in the butter and continue to shake the pan until the butter melts completely and coats all the potatoes (this will keep them from becoming sticky when they are mashed). Pour in the milk and heat until it begins to boil.

Third, remove the potatoes from heat. Use a potato masher or stiff wire whip to thoroughly mash the potatoes in an up-and-down motion. Beat in the egg with a wooden spoon, then season with a little salt and pepper. Fold in 1 1/2 cups of the grated cheddar cheese.

Fourth, butter a 1 1/2-quart ovenproof baking dish. Use a rubber spatula to spread the potato mixture evenly in the dish. Bake for 20 to 25 minutes.

Fifth, sprinkle the remaining 1/2 cup of cheese over the potatoes. Increase the oven temperature to 400°F and bake for an additional 15 minutes. Serve immediately.

STONE-GROUND CORN MUFFINS

12 Muffins ▪▪▪▪▪▪▪▪▪▪▪▪▪▪▪▪▪▪▪▪▪▪▪▪▪▪▪▪▪▪▪▪▪▪▪▪▪

Where breakfast muffins tend to be sweet, these are more savory—a bit like corn bread. And while golden squares of corn bread are a perennial favorite, corn muffins give you that toasted crunch on every side.

1/2 **cup shortening**

1/4 **cup granulated sugar**

2 **large eggs, room temperature**

I **cup all-purpose flour**

I **tablespoon baking powder**

1/2 **teaspoon salt**

I 1/2 **cups stone-ground cornmeal,
    divided**

I **cup whole milk**

Oven temperature 400°F.

First, butter 12 standard muffin cups (each about 1/2-cup capacity).

Second, thoroughly cream the shortening and sugar on high speed using an electric mixer fitted with a paddle. Turn the motor down to medium speed and add in the eggs one at a time, beating well to incorporate after each addition.

Third, sift the flour, baking powder, and salt into a separate bowl. Add in 3/4 cup of the cornmeal and whisk thoroughly to combine.

Fourth, beat together half of the flour mixture with the milk in a separate bowl. With the mixer on low speed, blend the batter into the shortening mixture.

Fifth, scrape down the sides of the bowl with a rubber spatula and gently fold in the remaining flour mixture. (Note: Do not overmix or the muffins will be tough.) Fold in the remaining 3/4 cup cornmeal.

Sixth, fill the muffin cups 3/4 full. Bake until the tops are golden and beginning to crack, 15 to 18 minutes. Cool the muffins in their tin for 5 minutes, and then turn out onto a cooling rack.

GARDEN PEA *and* CABBAGE SALAD

I doubt there is a better way to enjoy the sweet flavor of peas than when they are complemented by crunchy cabbage, green onions, and sour cream dressing.

SALAD

2 cups fresh blanched peas or frozen peas, thawed

4 cups shredded green or Savoy cabbage

1/2 cup diced celery

1/4 cup chopped scallions

1/2 teaspoon salt

DRESSING

1 cup sour cream

1/2 cup mayonnaise

2 teaspoons Dijon mustard

1 teaspoon white wine or cider vinegar

Make the salad: Combine the peas, cabbage, celery, and scallions in a decorative salad bowl. Sprinkle the salt over the vegetables and toss together well.

Prepare the dressing: Use a stiff wire whisk to blend the sour cream with the mayonnaise, mustard, and vinegar in a stainless mixing bowl.

To serve: Use a rubber spatula to gently fold the dressing into the vegetables.

HONEY-HAZELNUT ACORN SQUASH

8 Servings ▪▪▪▪▪ ▪▪▪ ▪ ▪ ▪ ▪▪ ▪ ▪ ▪ ▪ ▪ ▪ ▪ ▪

Baked squash is one of the many dishes the American Indians introduced to European settlers. In turn, Europeans introduced honey to America. I love the nutty aroma that is brought out when squash is roasted. It is even more wonderful with the addition of hazelnuts, brown sugar, and honey.

2 medium acorn squash

1 tablespoon vegetable oil

1/2 cup hazelnuts

1/2 cup (1 stick) butter

1/4 cup packed brown sugar

1/4 cup honey

Pinch of allspice

Oven temperature 350°F.

First, use a sharp knife to cut the squash in half. Remove the seeds and clean out any membrane. Rub each half with a little vegetable oil.

Second, place the squash halves, cut sides down, in an ovenproof baking dish. Bake until the squash are tender, about 30 minutes.

Third, coarsely chop the hazelnuts in a food processor fitted with a steel blade. Add the butter and brown sugar, and pulse to blend.

Fourth, when the squash are tender, carefully turn over so the rind sides are down, then spoon an equal amount of the hazelnut butter into the centers.

Fifth, drizzle the squash with the honey and dust with a pinch of allspice; then bake for an additional 10 minutes.

To serve: Quarter the squash and place on a platter. Pour all of the sweet drizzle from the baking dish over top. Serve immediately.

FARMHOUSE RHUBARB LATTICE PIE

8 Servings ■ ▪ ■ ▪ ■ ▪ ■ ▪ ■ ▪ ■ ▪ ■ ▪ ■ ▪ ■ ▪ ■ ▪ ■ ▪ ■ ▪ ■

Rhubarb arrives in early spring and in cooler climates lasts through the summer growing season and into early fall. People often enjoy rhubarb combined with strawberries during the summer or with apples in autumn. Both options are wonderful; you can substitute an equal quantity of sliced strawberries or apples for 1 to 2 cups of the rhubarb and reduce the sugar just a bit. I think you'll agree, though, that this homey pie is just fine as it is!

PIE CRUST

2 1/4 cups all-purpose flour

I teaspoon salt

3/4 cup shortening

6 to 7 tablespoons cold water

RHUBARB FILLING

5 cups sliced rhubarb (about 6 medium stalks)

6 rounded tablespoons all-purpose flour

I 1/2 cups granulated sugar

1/8 teaspoon salt

STREUSEL TOPPING

2 tablespoons unsalted butter

I tablespoon all-purpose flour

1/4 cup packed brown sugar

Oven temperature 400°F.

Make the pie crust: First, whisk the flour and salt together in a mixing bowl. Cut in the shortening with a pastry cutter until the mixture reaches the consistency of coarse crumbly meal.

Second, turn the mixture out onto a clean dry surface and knead in just enough of the cold water for the dough to come together in a pliable, tender ball. Divide the dough into two equal portions and roll into balls. Flatten each ball into a disk by gently pressing it between your hands. Wrap each disk in plastic wrap and chill for at least 30 minutes and up to 1 week.

Make the filling: Trim away any dry or woody ends from the rhubarb stalks and slice enough of the rhubarb into 3/4-inch-thick slices to yield 5 cups. Place the rhubarb slices in a stainless mixing bowl and toss together with the flour, sugar,

and salt. Allow the mixture to stand at room temperature for 20 to 25 minutes.

Make the streusel topping: Cut the butter, flour, and sugar together with a pastry cutter until the mixture is the consistency of coarse crumbly meal. Set aside.

Assemble the pie: First, when the pie dough has chilled for at least 30 minutes, roll out the bottom crust on a clean, lightly floured surface to a 1/4-inch thick 10-inch circle. Line the inside of a 10-inch pie plate with this crust. Shape the second piece of dough into a square. Roll it out in a 12-inch square and cut into 18 3/4-inch-wide strips.

Second, toss the rhubarb mixture together again so that the juices from the fruit are fully combined with the sugar and flour. Spoon the filling into the crust and sprinkle the streusel over the top. Lay the strips of dough alternately 1 inch apart, beginning in the middle of the pie circle. Fold back the strips as you weave them over and under to create a lattice pattern. Trim and crimp the crust edges.

Third, sprinkle the top of the crust with a little sugar and bake until the crust is golden and the filling is bubbling through the lattice top, 45 to 50 minutes.

Easy Time-Saving and Do-Ahead Tips

SATURDAY:

- Prepare the pie dough and refrigerate. Prepare the vegetables and the dressing for the salad and refrigerate separately.

- Bake the rhubarb pie.

SUNDAY MORNING:

- Prepare the meatloaf mixture for baking.

- Prepare the acorn squash and the potato casserole for baking.

- Butter the muffin tins and prepare the corn muffin batter.

Chapter 3

SAVORING SIMPLICITY

SAVORY CHICKEN *and* DUMPLINGS

SWEET CORN *and* LIMA BEAN SUCCOTASH

ICED RELISH TRAY *with* CELERY
SEED DRESSING

COCONUT CREAM CAKE

Often it is the simple things in life we savor most: a quiet walk, a beautiful sunset, a good book by a crackling fire, a gentle summer rain. The memory of one special dish, understated, completely sublime, and unpretentious in its making and presentation, is another. Sunday dinner can evoke those same feelings. And chicken and dumplings must certainly be among the simplest and most savory of Sunday dinners.

Chicken and dumplings can be found in almost every style of regional American cookery: from the heart of the South to the heart of New Jersey; from the Louisiana Bayou to the Texas panhandle; across the Ozarks and the high Western plains; around Memphis and Chicago; from the great northern lakes to the great Northwest woods. Wherever Americans gather to say grace, the homey appeal of this simple stew makes it a Sunday dinner favorite. Indeed, it would be difficult to find a nineteenth- or early-twentieth-century family cookbook in which chicken and dumplings do not appear.

The exact origin of chicken and dumplings is uncertain. Stewed poultry, or fricassee, as well as light and melting dumplings are hallmarks of central European cookery such as that found in the Czech Republic, Hungary, Poland, and Ukraine. The word *dumpling* itself, probably a variation of lump, is English. And African Americans, especially those whose ancestry is rooted in the Ivory Coast and Congo, where the family pot simmered all day, may well have contributed this classic to Southern cuisine. Then there were the Swiss, the Germans, and the Irish—almost everyone, it seems, brought some variation of chicken and dumplings to the American Sunday table.

Each family recipe, in fact, is unique. In most recipes the broth is thickened with just flour or cornstarch, but other recipes call for egg yolks and cream, which is a rich and wonderful variation. Dumplings can be made with broth, milk, or buttermilk, bound with eggs, lightened with baking powder, and "cut in" with chicken fat, butter, or shortening. They can be rolled and cut like wide noodles, dropped like biscuits, pinched from soft dough, shaped into little ovals, or cut into thick squares called slick dumplings. They can be cooked after the chicken has been removed from the broth, steamed on top of the chicken, or baked atop the stew like a cobbler crust. The dish can be served like a casserole or presented in bowls with fat juicy pieces of chicken sitting beneath the savory dumplings and sauce.

So which of these is the authentic, all-American chicken and dumplings? All of them. No wonder this has been a Sunday dinner favorite throughout the country.

Savory Chicken and Dumplings

Serves 8

Chicken:
2 large chicken and turkey thighs
2 cups chicken stock
1 carrot, peeled and finely sliced
2 ribs celery with leaves, finely sliced
1 small onion, quartered
thyme
sage

...when the chicken...
...cold water to cover...
...teaspoon old bay season...
onion, thyme and sage; bring to
reduce heat to low; cover,
and simmer until the ch...
About 1 Hour.

Dumplings:
2 cups all-purpose flour
1 tablespoon baking po...
1/2 teaspoon white pepp...
1/2 teaspoon dry mus...
1/2 teaspoon salt
2 large eggs; room...

SAVORY CHICKEN *and* DUMPLINGS

8 Servings

On the nineteenth-century farm, chickens were kept for laying eggs; when they became too old and were too tough for frying or baking, they went into the pot for a soup or stew. While stewing a chicken may no longer be necessary for a tender dish, the simple, savory flavor is hard to beat. I prefer using only thighs for this dish. The key to light, wonderful dumplings is a tight-fitting lid for the pot. Drop the dumplings in the pot, and then cover until they are done. Resist the temptation to have a look inside while they're cooking—it's a test of faith!

CHICKEN

8 large chicken thighs

2 cups chicken broth

1 carrot, peeled and thinly sliced

2 ribs celery with leaves, thinly sliced

1 small onion, quartered

1 sprig of thyme

Pinch of rubbed sage

DUMPLINGS

2 cups all-purpose flour

1 tablespoon baking powder

1/2 teaspoon dry rubbed sage

1 teaspoon salt

1/2 teaspoon white pepper

2 large eggs, room temperature

2 tablespoons rendered chicken fat or shortening

2/3 cup whole milk

6 cups cooking liquid from the chicken; plus additional chicken broth, if needed

 ### GRAVY

3 cups cooking liquid from the chicken plus additional chicken broth, if needed

1 chicken bouillon cube or 1 tablespoon concentrated chicken stock

1/4 cup all-purpose flour

1 cup half-and-half

Salt and white pepper to taste

Stew the chicken: Thoroughly rinse the chicken thighs under cold running water; then pat dry. Place the chicken in a single layer, skin side up, in the bottom of a large covered sauté pan or Dutch oven. Pour in the chicken broth, as well as enough cold water to just cover the chicken, about 4 cups. Add in the carrot, celery, onion, thyme, and sage. Bring to a boil over high heat, reduce the heat to low, cover the pan and simmer until the chicken is tender and nearly falling from the bones, about 1 hour.

Make the dumplings: First, whisk together the flour, baking powder, sage, salt, and white pepper in a mixing bowl.

Second, combine the eggs with the chicken fat or shortening in a separate bowl. Whisk together until the shortening is broken into little bits and has partially blended with the eggs. Whisk in the milk, leaving the little bits of shortening floating on the surface.

Third, use a fork to blend the dry ingredients into the egg mixture 1/2 cup at a time. Once the mixture is too stiff to blend with the fork, knead with the tips of your fingers just enough to incorporate the remaining flour. The dough will be fairly light, moist, and a little sticky. Wrap the dough in plastic and refrigerate for at least 30 minutes and up to 4 hours.

Assemble the chicken and dumplings: First, dust the dough with a little flour, divide into 2 pieces, and roll each piece on a lightly floured work surface into a 2-inch-round log. Use a sharp knife to slice each log into 8 biscuit-size pieces.

Second, remove the tender chicken thighs from the broth with a slotted spoon, transfer to a warm serving platter, and tent with foil to keep warm. Strain the broth through a fine sieve and add in enough extra chicken broth to measure 6 cups. Return to high heat until the broth begins to bubble vigorously; then place the dumplings directly into the stock. Gently lift the dumplings with a fork to make sure they do not stick to the bottom. Reduce the heat to medium-low, cover with a tight-fitting lid and cook undisturbed for 12 to 15 minutes. The dumplings will soak up a little more than half the liquid and double in size as they cook.

Make the gravy: First, transfer the dumplings to the warm serving platter alongside the chicken. Strain the liquid and add in enough chicken broth to measure 3 cups. Return the liquid to the pot and increase the heat to medium. Add the bouillon cube to the simmering broth.

Second, whisk the flour and half-and-half in a small bowl until completely smooth, then slowly add to the simmering broth, stirring constantly. Continue stirring until the gravy thickens, about 3 minutes. Adjust the seasoning to taste with salt and white pepper.

To serve: Pour the gravy over the chicken and dumplings, and serve immediately. Pass any extra gravy in a gravy boat.

SWEET CORN *and* LIMA BEAN SUCCOTASH

8 Servings ■ ▬ ▬ ■ ▬ ■ ▬ ▬ ▬ ■ ▬ ▬ ■ ▬ ■ ▬ ■ ▬ ■ ▬ ■ ▬

Succotash is a dish of American Indian origin that became a favorite in early colonial cookery. It was originally served as a main dish—corn and lima beans cooked with wild game. Puritans had no taste for game, which in England was reserved for royalty, so they began using salt pork and chicken. In the South and eventually the Midwest, succotash became a vegetable dish like this one. Its variations are still passionately debated in New England, where an annual Succotash Festival is held.

1/4 **cup (1/2 stick) butter**

1/2 **cup thinly sliced onion**

2 cups fresh blanched lima beans or frozen lima beans, thawed

2 cups fresh steamed corn or frozen corn, thawed

I **teaspoon granulated sugar**

I **cup half-and-half**

Salt and white pepper to taste

First, melt the butter in a skillet over medium heat. Add in the sliced onion and sauté until translucent, 2 to 3 minutes. Add in the lima beans and the corn, and sauté for 2 more minutes, being careful not to let the butter brown. Season with the sugar.

Second, pour in the half-and-half and bring to a simmer; cook until the vegetables have absorbed most of the liquid, the dish is slightly thickened, and the vegetables are tender, about 10 minutes. Season to taste with salt and white pepper. Serve immediately.

ICED RELISH TRAY *with* CELERY SEED DRESSING

8 Servings

The relish tray was once a pretty standard addition to the American table, even in formal circles at the finest white-tablecloth restaurants—I miss that. I think it's time that custom made a comeback.

RELISH TRAY

1 bunch green onions

1 bunch radishes

1 (8-ounce) package baby carrots

4 ribs celery, cut into 3-inch sticks

1 (12-ounce) jar bread-and-butter
  pickles

1 (12-ounce) jar pickled okra

DRESSING

1/2 cup minced sweet onion

1/4 cup granulated sugar

1/4 cup cider vinegar

1/2 teaspoon celery seeds

1 teaspoon dry mustard

1/4 teaspoon salt

1/3 cup vegetable oil

Prepare the vegetables: Snip the root ends from the green onions and trim any wilted green tops. Trim the root ends and green tops from the radishes. Place the green onions, radishes, carrots, and celery in a bowl of ice water for 1 hour before dinner so they will be icy cold and crunchy.

Make the dressing: Combine the onion, sugar, and vinegar in a saucepan. Stir over medium-high heat until the sugar is dissolved and the onion is soft, about 2 minutes. Whisk in the celery seeds, mustard, and salt. Purée the mixture in a blender. Slowly pour in the oil and continue to purée until the dressing is smooth. Cover with plastic wrap and chill until ready to serve.

Serve the relish tray: Drain the ice water from the raw vegetables and shake off any excess water. Arrange the vegetables with the pickles and pickled okra on a decorative platter with an accompanying dish of dressing and a small ladle. (Note: It's nice to have 2 or more relish trays within easy reach on each end of the table, to avoid passing all the way to the other end.)

COCONUT CREAM CAKE

New desserts may come and go, but we keep returning to savor the simple, elegant creations that we fondly remember and always enjoy. There are, of course, untold variations on this Southern classic. My grandmother's recipe was a basic 1, 2, 3 , 4 cake (1 cup of butter, 2 cups of sugar, 3 cups of flour, and 4 eggs)—flavored with cream of coconut and topped with an equally classic, sweet and gooey coconut-infused 7-minute frosting.

CAKE

3 cups cake flour

4 teaspoons baking powder

$1/2$ teaspoon salt

I cup unsalted butter

2 cups granulated sugar

$1/2$ teaspoon pure coconut extract

I teaspoon pure vanilla extract

4 large egg yolks, room temperature

$1/2$ cup whole milk

$1/2$ cup cream of coconut (such as Coco Lopez)

FROSTING

3 large egg whites, room temperature

3/4 cup granulated sugar

$1/3$ cup cream of coconut

$1/8$ teaspoon cream of tartar

$1/2$ teaspoon pure coconut extract

I cup flaked sweetened coconut

Oven temperature 350°F.

Make the cake layers: First, grease and lightly flour two 9-inch round cake pans with 2-inch sides.

Second, sift together the cake flour, baking powder, and salt in a large bowl and set aside.

Third, combine the butter and sugar in the bowl of a mixer fitted with a paddle. Cream together on medium-high speed for 6 to 8 minutes, until light and fluffy. Turn the mixer off and scrape down the sides of the bowl with a rubber spatula, then add in the coconut extract.

Fourth, lower the mixer speed to medium-low. Add in the egg yolks one at a time, mixing well after each addition.

Fifth, turn the mixer speed down to low. Add the sifted dry ingredients alternately with the milk and coconut cream in 3 batches, beating slowly but thoroughly after each addition to fully incorporate all of the ingredients. Do not overmix.

Sixth, divide the batter evenly between the prepared pans. Place the pans on a middle oven rack and bake for 30 minutes. The cakes are done when they begin to pull away from the edges of the pan and spring back when pressed gently in the center. Allow the layers to cool in the pans for 10 minutes on wire racks. Then carefully run a thin sharp knife around the inside edge of each pan to loosen. Turn the cake layers out onto a cooling rack.

Prepare the frosting: First, combine 3 egg whites with the sugar, coconut cream, and cream of tartar in a stainless mixing bowl or in the top of a double boiler. Dissolve the sugar by beating for about 1 minute with a handheld electric mixer running on high speed.

Second, place over a pan of rapidly boiling water and continue to beat until soft peaks form, about 7 minutes.

Third, remove the bowl from over the boiling water. Add in the coconut extract and continue beating until the frosting reaches spreading consistency, 2 to 3 minutes. Allow the frosting to cool completely.

Assemble the cake: Place 1 layer of the cake on a serving platter or cake stand. Use an icing spatula or table knife to spread about 1/3 of the frosting evenly on the cake. Sprinkle the frosting with 1/3 of the coconut flakes. Place the second layer over the first, and cover the top and sides of the cake with the remaining frosting; sprinkle with the remaining sweetened coconut flakes. Cover the cake with a dome or bowl and keep at room temperature for up to one day before serving.

Easy Time-Saving and Do-Ahead Tips

SATURDAY:

- Bake and frost the coconut cream cake. Store covered at room temperature.

- Prepare the celery seed dressing and refrigerate.

- Prepare the vegetables for the relish tray and succotash; refrigerate in well-sealed containers.

SUNDAY MORNING:

- Prepare the dumpling dough and refrigerate.

Chapter 4

A QUIET SUNDAY
with FRIENDS

SLOW-COOKED BEEF BRISKET
with MUSHROOMS, RED BEETS,
and PEARL ONIONS

PENNSYLVANIA DUTCH EGG SPAETZLE

AMISH POTATO ROLLS

BUTTERED BRUSSELS SPROUTS
with PARSLEY *and* CHIVES

BAKED APPLES *with* WALNUTS *and* CREAM

For a beautiful look at the simple life, why not try a quiet Sunday ride through Lancaster County in southeast Pennsylvania? Life here moves at a slower pace than you might be accustomed to. The clip-clop of horses' hooves echoes along the country roads, across covered wooden bridges spanning quiet streams, and past rolling green hills and tidy farms, where windmills turn faithfully in the gentle breeze. The buggies are horse drawn, mule teams plow the fields, and the dress is simple for those who call themselves the "plain people." These are the Amish and Mennonites who first came to this area centuries ago to take advantage of William Penn's "holy experiment."

Penn, an English Quaker, established Pennsylvania in 1682, when he received the lands from the English crown in payment for a debt. He had been imprisoned numerous times for his religious beliefs and was determined to use his newly acquired property to create something new: a society built on pacifism, equality for all peoples, and religious tolerance. He and his Quaker followers, who called themselves Friends, named their capital Philadelphia, meaning "city of brotherly love." Together they established a charter offering an almost unprecedented freedom of belief.

The German-speaking settlers that became known as the Pennsylvania Dutch—a misunderstanding of Deutsch, their word for German—are found throughout this beautiful region. Unadorned clothing, avoidance of modern conveniences, strict pacifism, and a close community life characterized these settlements. Like the Quakers, they conducted worship services in homes or in simple meeting houses—a gathering of friends, followed by a Sabbath Day dinner—traditions that continue to the present day.

My wife and I travel to Pennsylvania quite often to visit friends. We enjoy wandering around the many art and craft festivals, farmer's markets, and the Amish stores. Here you can still find hand-crafted quilts, hand-made furniture, and home-made candies. Whether in the big cities, small towns, or at some rural crossroads, the farmers' markets offer crisp, tart, juicy apples, dairy-rich cream and butter, fresh-from-the-garden vegetables, and an abundance of mushrooms. (Pennsylvania is the world's largest mushroom producer.)

Slowly simmered meats, rich egg noodles or dumpling, and delicious fruit-filled desserts are the hallmarks of this region—dishes that reflect the time-honored traditions of the people who long settled here. From this simple abundance and rich history comes a hearty and satisfying menu—a menu that bids us to the Sunday table for a quiet dinner with friends.

SLOW-COOKED BEEF BRISKET *with* MUSHROOMS, RED BEETS, *and* PEARL ONIONS

8 Servings

Braised brisket is slow-cooked, just like any great pot roast. I prefer to use a nice variety of mushrooms as an accompaniment. For the dark vinegar I use balsamic, which is readily available throughout the country. The inclusion of red beets and onions creates a dark-hued gravy with a remarkably earthy flavor.

BEEF BRISKET

1 (4- to 5-pound) beef brisket, excess fat trimmed, about 2 inches thick

Salt and pepper

Vegetable oil to season the pan

1/2 cup balsamic vinegar

2 cups beef broth

1/2 cup dark raisins

2 sprigs fresh thyme

VEGETABLES

4 large red beets

2 pounds assorted mushrooms

16 ounces (1 dry pint) red pearl onions, peeled

Pinch of salt

GRAVY

3 tablespoons all-purpose flour

1/4 cup water

Salt and pepper to taste

Oven temperature 300°F.

Make the brisket: First, season the meat by rubbing it with salt and pepper.

Second, pour in just enough oil to coat the bottom of a Dutch oven or braising pan fitted with a lid. Heat the oil over medium-high heat until it just begins to smoke. Reduce the heat slightly and brown the meat on all sides, beginning with the leanest side, turning it every minute or so for about 10 minutes.

Third, when the meat is browned on all sides, place it in the center of the pan with the fat side up, and then pour in the vinegar. Fit the lid onto the pan and simmer for 5 minutes, then reduce the temperature of the burner to low. Pour in the beef broth and enough water to cover the brisket a little less than halfway, and add in the raisins and the thyme sprigs. Then replace the lid and allow the meat to simmer slowly over low heat on the stovetop or in a 300°F oven for about 2 hours.

Prepare the vegetables: First, peel the beets, leaving about an inch of the tops, if desired. Cut the beets into quarters. Clean the mushrooms under cool running water to remove any soil, then remove and discard any woody stems. Cut the mushrooms into halves, quarters, or thick slices.

Second, when the brisket has simmered for about 2 hours, place it over medium heat. Add the beets to the liquid surrounding the roast and simmer for 15 minutes. Add in a little more water, if needed; then add in the onions and the mushrooms so they cover both the roast and the beets. Season

them with a pinch of salt. Replace the lid and return the casserole dish to the oven or place over low heat on the stovetop and cook for 45 minutes.

Third, when the brisket is done cooking, the meat should be tender, just falling away from the fat, but still firm enough to slice easily. Transfer the brisket to a clean cutting board and allow it to rest for 15 minutes. Use a slotted spoon to transfer the beets, mushrooms, onions, and raisins from the Dutch oven to a bowl. Remove and discard the thyme sprigs. Turn the burner to medium-high and prepare the gravy.

Make the gravy: In a small bowl blend the flour with water and use a stiff wire whisk to form a smooth paste. When the liquid remaining in the Dutch oven begins to simmer, add in about half of the paste as you whisk constantly. Add more paste, a little at a time, until the gravy has thickened. Turn the heat to low and allow the gravy to simmer for 5 minutes, and then season to taste with salt and pepper.

To serve: Place the brisket on a platter and artfully arrange the beets, mushrooms, and onions around it. Lace the platter with some of the gravy. Pass the extra gravy separately in a gravy boat.

PENNSYLVANIA DUTCH EGG SPAETZLE

8 Servings ▪▪▪▪▪▪▪▪▪▪▪▪▪▪▪▪▪▪▪▪▪▪▪▪▪▪

Spaetzle are little dumplings made from fresh egg pasta, and they are traditionally served with pot roast, brisket, or short ribs. They are easy to prepare and quite delicious. The trick is to make the batter an hour ahead and have a ready pot of boiling water that is large enough to keep the little bits of batter from sticking to one another as they cook.

4 large eggs, room temperature, lightly beaten

2 cups whole milk

Pinch of nutmeg

1 teaspoon salt

Pinch of ground pepper

4 cups all-purpose flour

1/2 cup (1 stick) butter

First, add the eggs and milk to a large bowl and beat using a stiff wire whisk. Add in the nutmeg, salt, and pepper. Use a wooden spoon to mix in the flour, 1 cup at a time, beating well after each addition until the mixture is smooth and elastic. The mixture should now be the consistency of thick, slightly elastic pancake batter. Let the spaetzle batter stand at room temperature for 1 hour.

Meanwhile, bring a large pot of cool salted water to a boil.

Second, suspend a large-holed colander or spaetzle sieve about 6 inches over the top of the boiling water. Try a test batch by first putting a couple of tablespoons of the spaetzle batter through the colander into the boiling water—if it runs quickly through the colander, add a little flour, a tablespoon at a time, to thicken the batter; if you have to press down hard to push the batter through the holes, add a little milk.

Third, working in 4 separate batches, pour the dough into the colander, pressing it through the holes with a rubber spatula (the droplets will form little "dumplings"). When the first little dumplings begin to float, stir the water gently to keep them from sticking together. Cook the spaetzle until tender, 4 to 5 minutes.

Meanwhile, prepare a large bowl of cold water to cool the spaetzle in.

Fourth, carefully remove the spaetzle from the boiling water using a large slotted spoon or small strainer and immediately submerge in the cold water. When all of the spaetzle have cooled, drain thoroughly and transfer to a glass or stainless bowl. The spaetzle can be prepared a day ahead up to this point—toss them in a little vegetable oil, cover tightly with plastic wrap, and refrigerate.

Fifth, transfer the spaetzle to a colander and run under hot water for a minute, then shake off the excess water. Heat a nonstick skillet over medium-high heat. Cut the butter into pats and quickly add them to the hot skillet so that they melt all at once. Add the cooked spaetzle to the melted butter and toss continually with a wooden spoon to keep them from sticking to the bottom of the skillet; sauté for 1 minute so that the spaetzle can absorb the butter. Serve immediately.

AMISH POTATO ROLLS

24 Rolls ▪▪

Potato breads are soft and densely textured (and a great way to use up leftover mashed potatoes). The ever-efficient Germans often used potato water to make natural yeast starters for bread. Incidentally, a variation of these rolls can be found accompanying another German-influenced American dish—the hamburger.

2 medium potatoes, scrubbed and peeled

$1/2$ cup reserved warm potato water (about 110°F)

2 tablespoons granulated sugar

1 package (2 $1/4$ teaspoons) active dry yeast

$1/4$ cup ($1/2$ stick) unsalted butter

$2/3$ cup whole milk

1 teaspoon salt

1 large egg, room temperature, lightly beaten

4 $1/2$ cups all-purpose flour, sifted

Oven temperature 400°F.

First, cook the potatoes in boiling salted water until they are tender when pierced with a fork. Drain them completely, reserving $1/2$ cup of the potato water. Cool the potato water to lukewarm. Mash the potatoes and measure out 1 cup for making the rolls. Cool the mashed potatoes to room temperature.

Second, dissolve the sugar in the lukewarm potato water and sprinkle the yeast over the surface. Let the yeast mixture stand until it becomes foamy, about 5 minutes; then stir to dissolve.

Third, combine the butter, milk, and salt in a small heavy-bottomed saucepan and heat until the butter is just melted. Remove from the heat and use a wooden spoon to mix in the 1 cup of reserved mashed potatoes. Add in the lightly beaten egg, then the dissolved yeast.

Fourth, transfer the dough to the bowl of a mixer fitted with a dough hook. Slowly add in 4 cups of the sifted flour, 1 cup at a time, scraping down the sides of the bowl after each addition. Knead on low speed until the dough is smooth and elastic, 4 to 5 minutes. Then cover the bowl with a clean tea towel and set it in a draft-free place until it has doubled in size, about 1 hour.

Fifth, punch the dough down. Knead in the remaining 1/2 cup flour, as needed. The dough should be soft and slightly sticky, but firm enough to just hold its shape. Cover the bowl with a clean tea towel and allow it to rise in a draft-free place for another 30 minutes. (Note: At this point you can refrigerate the dough for up to 2 hours before shaping the rolls.)

Sixth, place the dough on a clean cutting board that has been dusted with a little flour and divide into 2 dozen equal pieces. Dust each piece with a little more flour and roll into a ball.

Seventh, place the balls about 1 inch apart on a well-greased baking sheet. Cover the pan with a clean tea towel and let the rolls rise for another 15 to 20 minutes (or for about 40 minutes if the dough was refrigerated). When the rolls have risen, use a pastry brush to lightly brush the tops of the rolls with a little milk, and then bake them for 10 to 12 minutes.

BUTTERED BRUSSELS SPROUTS
with PARSLEY *and* CHIVES

8 Servings

Tender baby Brussels sprouts are the best choice when available, so look for nice small ones that are deep green with tight firm leaves.

2 pounds Brussels sprouts, trimmed and halved

6 tablespoons (3/4 stick) butter

Salt to taste

1 tablespoon fresh snipped chives

1/2 tablespoon fresh chopped parsley

First, bring a large pot of salted water to a full boil. Drop the Brussels sprouts into the water and cook them until they are bright green and tender, about 8 minutes. Drain the sprouts thoroughly.

Second, melt the butter in a small skillet over low heat; when the butter begins to bubble, add in the sprouts and season to taste with salt. Cover the skillet with a tight-fitting lid and steam for 3 to 4 minutes. Just before serving, toss in the chives and parsley.

BAKED APPLES *with* WALNUTS *and* CREAM

8 Servings ■ ▪

*This is one of my very favorite childhood desserts. It is best to use crisp, sweet-tart apples,
such as Cox Pippin, McIntosh, Winesap, or Jonathans.*

8 medium sweet-tart apples

1 cup chopped walnuts

1 cup packed dark brown sugar

1/2 teaspoon allspice

1 teaspoon cinnamon

1/2 cup (1 stick) unsalted butter

**2/3 cup apple cider, room
temperature**

1 quart heavy cream

Oven temperature 350°F.

First, wash, dry and core the apples.

Second, combine the chopped walnuts, brown sugar, allspice, and cinnamon in a small bowl. Fill the center of each apple with an equal amount of this mixture and place it into a deep baking pan. The pan should be large enough to ensure that the apples do not touch one another.

Third, dot the top of each apple with 1 tablespoon of butter, pour the apple cider over the apples and sprinkle with any remaining filling. Bake them for 45 to 50 minutes. The apples are done when the skin is just beginning to split around the top and they are easily pierced with a knife.

Fourth, remove the apples from the oven and baste them with the pan syrup. Transfer each apple to an individual serving bowl. Spoon the remaining syrup from the bottom of the pan and 1/2 cup heavy cream over each apple and top with the remaining heavy cream. Serve immediately.

Chapter 5

SWEET COMFORT
and SOUL

BRAISED COUNTRY GREENS

BONELESS SMOTHERED PORK CHOPS

TWICE-BAKED SWEET POTATO CASSEROLE

SUNDAY COMFORT MACARONI *and* CHEESE

BANANA BLACK-BOTTOM CREAM PIE

Sunday is a day to rejoice. It is a day for praise. It is a day for folks to gather together. The soul of Sunday dinner is found in the sweet comfort of fellowship and friendship. For Americans of African heritage, Sunday dinner is a tradition for both family and extended family.

By the end of the eighteenth century, a large native-born population of African-Americans began to emerge. With that came the desire to establish churches that met the unique needs of slaves and former slaves. In 1787, two freed slaves in Pennsylvania, Richard Allen and Absalom Jones, began a benevolent organization called the Free African Society. In 1794 Reverend Allen, responding to the "unkind treatment" of his fellow blacks in their Methodist Church, founded what would eventually become the African Methodist Episcopal Church. The AME and other African American churches became important centers of community and culture, offering education and hope along with spiritual comfort and release.

Just as church became a place of refuge from oppression and a center for struggle against slavery and social injustice, Sunday became a day for strengthening community ties, for strengthening family bonds, and for celebrating a shared history. As Sunday became an important day for black families across the country, Sunday dinner became an important meal and an important celebration.

Every recipe tells a story, and these stories—our families' oral histories—are passed down from generation to generation. These stories are not just shared around the family table but around the kitchen. Indeed, it is often the casual conversations, shared through laughter and tears and around a common task, that we remember most. Preparing a meal together passes on more than just kitchen skill and recipes; it passes on our heritage.

The African American influence on our cuisine, like the influence of gospel music on our culture, has been profound. "Soul food," a term coined in the 1960s to refer to African American home-style cooking, began as a slave's diet. It is a mix of cooking styles blended with African ingredients and indigenous foods. Corn and sweet potatoes, first introduced to African soil in the sixteenth century by Portuguese traders, returned to our shores, along with vegetables such as okra, black-eyed peas, yams, and the exotic fruits found in the Caribbean. Add to that the regional influences of West Indian, Caribbean, and French cooking, and you have a cuisine that is the essence of comfort.

BRAISED COUNTRY GREENS

Collard, mustard, and turnip greens each have a spicy snap. The secret to cooking greens is to cook them just enough to become tender yet still retain a bit of crunch. It is a good idea to keep the seasonings simple so that the natural flavor of the greens is enhanced, not overwhelmed. I like to season the greens with salted country ham. Although 3 pounds may seem like a lot of greens, they quickly cook down.

3 pounds fresh assorted greens

4 ounces country ham or bacon

1 tablespoon cider vinegar

1 cup chopped green onions

Salt, pepper, and cayenne to taste

First, wash the greens thoroughly in several changes of cool running water, removing any wilted or brown leaves. Dry the leaves and wash again, this time leaving the leaves wet—what water remains on the leaves is enough to steam them. Set aside.

Second, dice the ham or bacon, including all the bits of fat, and sauté in a heavy-bottomed skillet over medium heat just long enough to render the fat, about 2 minutes. Add the collard greens to the pan first, as they take just a little longer to cook. Let them cook down for 2 to 3 minutes, then add in the other greens. Cover the skillet with a tight-fitting lid and wilt the greens over medium heat, tossing from time to time with the ham or bacon, for about 15 minutes.

Third, add in the vinegar and the green onions. Cook for 1 minute or so and then taste to test the seasoning. (Remember, country ham is quite salty.) Season to taste with salt, pepper, and cayenne. Continue to toss the greens over heat until they become tender, 1 to 2 minutes more. Serve immediately.

BONELESS SMOTHERED PORK CHOPS

8 Servings ■ ▪ ■ ▪ ■ ▪ ■ ▪ ■ ▪ ■ ▪ ■ ▪ ■ ▪ ■ ▪ ■ ▪ ■

These delicious, tender pork chops are first coated with seasoned bread crumbs and a tang of mustard, then lightly fried and finally baked in the oven for a crusty outside and juicy center. The lard adds a wonderful, unmatched flavor—with fewer calories than olive oil.

PORK CHOPS

1/2 cup all-purpose flour

1 teaspoon salt

1/2 teaspoon pepper

2 large eggs

1/4 cup prepared yellow mustard

1 cup fresh bread crumbs

2 tablespoons fresh chopped parsley

8 (1 to 1 1/2-inch-thick) boneless center-cut pork loin chops (6 to 8 ounces each)

1/4 cup lard or vegetable shortening

GRAVY

1/4 cup diced smoked bacon

2 cups thinly sliced onion

3 tablespoons all-purpose flour

2 tablespoons prepared yellow mustard

2 cups chicken broth

Tabasco sauce

Salt and pepper to taste

Oven temperature 350°F.

Make the pork chops: First, place the flour in a pie dish or on a large plate and season with the salt and pepper. Whisk the eggs into the mustard in a medium shallow bowl. Combine the bread crumbs with the parsley in a second pie dish or on another large plate.

Second, dredge the pork chops in the seasoned flour, shaking off any excess. Dip the chops into the egg mixture, then coat both sides with the bread crumbs. Transfer the chops to a clean platter as you work.

Third, melt the lard in a large ovenproof skillet over medium-high heat. The lard is hot enough if a pinch of flour sizzles when sprinkled in the pan. Place the breaded chops in the skillet and fry them until golden, turning once, about 2 minutes per side. When the chops are done, transfer the uncovered skillet to the oven. Bake until the chops are crisp on the outside and moist

and juicy in the middle, about 20 minutes; then remove the skillet from the oven and transfer the chops to a large serving platter. Tent the platter with foil to keep them warm.

Make the gravy: First, add the bacon to the skillet that the chops were in and cook over medium-high heat just long enough to render the fat, about 2 minutes. Add in the onion slices and continue cooking for 2 to 3 minutes more. As the bacon and onion cook, scrape the bottom of the skillet with a wire whisk to loosen any browned bits that might be sticking to the bottom of the pan.

Second, add the flour and mustard to the pan and whisk into a paste. Pour in the chicken broth, whisking to blend, then reduce the heat to medium-low and simmer until the gravy thickens, about 4 minutes. Add a dash of Tabasco sauce, and season to taste with salt and pepper.

To serve: Pour the gravy over the chops just before serving. If desired, garnish with fresh parsley sprigs.

TWICE-BAKED SWEET POTATO CASSEROLE

8 Servings ■ ▪ ▪ ■ ▪ ▪ ■ ▪ ▪ ■ ▪ ▪ ■ ▪ ■ ▪ ■ ▪ ■ ▪ ■ ▪ ■

This wonderful side dish is a perfect complement to pork. Baking sweet potatoes gives them a nutty, toasted flavor. And baking them twice, especially if you add in a little brown sugar, vanilla, and allspice, makes them even better.

SWEET POTATO CASSEROLE

3 pounds sweet potatoes

¹/₂ cup (1 stick) butter, softened

¹/₄ cup heavy cream

2 large eggs

¹/₄ cup packed light brown sugar

1 teaspoon pure vanilla extract

¹/₄ teaspoon allspice

Pinch of mace

Salt and pepper to taste

TOPPING

¹/₄ cup (¹/₂ stick) unsalted butter

¹/₄ cup packed light brown sugar

¹/₄ cup chopped pecans

Oven temperature 375°F.

First, scrub the sweet potatoes and prick their skins with a fork. Bake uncovered on a baking sheet until they are soft, about 1 hour. Allow the potatoes to cool, then peel away the skin using a sharp paring knife. Place the peeled potatoes in a mixing bowl and blend until smooth with a potato masher or stiff wire whisk.

Second, add the butter, cream, eggs, brown sugar, and vanilla to the mashed sweet potatoes and use a stiff wire whisk to whip together thoroughly. Add in the allspice and mace; then season to taste with salt and pepper.

Third, spoon the sweet potato mixture into a buttered baking dish, dot with pats of butter and sprinkle with the brown sugar and chopped pecans. Bake for 30 to 40 minutes. The sweet potatoes will puff up slightly and the topping will be bubbly and golden when the casserole is done.

SUNDAY COMFORT
MACARONI *and* CHEESE

8 Servings

Thomas Jefferson is credited with bringing pasta to the American table. Macaroni, which he served to guests at the White House, was a favorite. No doubt it was his slave-born and celebrated chef, James Hemings, who created most of the wonderful dishes for which Monticello was known. After learning French cuisine on his travels with then—French ambassador Jefferson, Hemings became one of the foremost influences in American cookery.

1 pound elbow macaroni

¼ cup (½ stick) butter

4 cups whole milk

16 slices American cheese

2 cups grated cheddar cheese

Tabasco sauce

Salt and pepper to taste

First, cook the macaroni in a large pot of boiling salted water until tender but firm (al dente), about 5 to 6 minutes. Drain through a colander, but do not rinse.

Second, add the macaroni back into the pot with the butter and stir until the butter melts and coats the macaroni. Pour in the milk and bring the mixture to a boil over medium heat; cook for 2 more minutes. Break the cheese slices into pieces, add in all the pieces at once and stir until the cheese is completely melted. The starch from the pasta will combine with the butter, milk, and cheese to form a rich, creamy sauce.

Third, stir in the grated cheddar cheese, add a dash of Tabasco, and season to taste with salt and pepper. If the cheese sauce is too thick for your liking, add extra milk, a tablespoon at a time, until it reaches the desired consistency. Transfer to a decorative bowl and serve immediately.

BANANA BLACK-BOTTOM CREAM PIE

8 Servings

This sensational pie is the perfect combination of bananas, dark chocolate, sweet vanilla, rum custard, and cream. You'll love the ease of making the Oreo cookie crust, which uses the whole cookie—filling and all! Make this wonderful pie a day ahead so the flavors can infuse and intensify.

OREO COOKIE CRUST

2 1/2 dozen Oreo cookies

5 tablespoons unsalted butter, melted

FILLING

1 tablespoon rum flavoring

2 teaspoons pure vanilla extract

1 teaspoon unflavored gelatin

6 ounces semisweet or bittersweet chocolate

2/3 cup granulated sugar

3 tablespoons cornstarch

1/4 teaspoon salt

3 cups half-and-half

4 large egg yolks, room temperature

1/4 cup (1/2 stick) unsalted butter

3 ripe medium bananas

1 pint heavy cream

1/3 cup granulated sugar

2 ounces semisweet or bittersweet chocolate, grated

Oven temperature 400°F.

Make the crust: Place the cookies (including the cream filling) in the bowl of a food processor fitted with a steel blade; blend just long enough to achieve fine crumbs. Add in the melted butter and pulse until completely combined. Press the mixture into the bottom and up the sides of a 2-inch-deep pie pan. Bake the crust for 10 minutes, then remove from the oven and cool.

Prepare the filling: First, combine the rum flavoring and vanilla in a small bowl. Sprinkle the gelatin on top and let the mixture stand for 10 minutes; then whisk together until smooth.

Second, finely chop the 6 ounces of chocolate and transfer to a separate larger bowl.

Third, whisk together 2/3 cup sugar, cornstarch, and salt in a heavy-bottomed saucepan and gradually add in the half-and-half and egg yolks, whisking lightly until smooth. Cook the mixture over medium-high heat, stirring constantly, until the custard is smooth, thick, and bubbling, 6 to 8 minutes.

Fourth, quickly add 1 1/4 cups of the hot custard into the chopped chocolate. Stir until the chocolate melts and the mixture is completely smooth. Immediately pour the chocolate filling into the baked crust and transfer to the freezer or refrigerator to cool, 5 to 10 minutes.

Meanwhile, add 1 cup of the remaining hot custard to the dissolved gelatin and stir until the

gelatin is evenly blended. Pour the gelatin mixture into the custard and whisk. Let the rum custard cool for about 5 minutes. Cut the butter into pats and whisk them into the custard until the butter is completely blended.

Fifth, cut the bananas into 1/2-inch-thick slices and toss the slices in a little rum or rum flavoring to prevent them from discoloring. Layer the slices of banana over the cooled chocolate custard in the cookie crust; then spoon the rum custard over the bananas and smooth the surface with a rubber spatula. Cut a 9-inch circle from a sheet of waxed paper, lightly coat it with butter, and place it directly on top of the custard to keep a skin from forming. Chill in the refrigerator until set, about 4 hours; then, without removing the waxed paper, cover the pie with plastic wrap and return to the refrigerator.

Assemble the pie: First, pour the cream into the chilled bowl of a mixer and add 1/3 cup sugar. Mix with a chilled balloon whisk at medium speed until the sugar has dissolved, 3 to 4 minutes. Then whip on high until stiff peaks hold, about 2 more minutes.

Second, carefully remove the waxed paper from the top of the pie. Mound the whipped cream over the custard with a rubber spatula, or use a pastry bag to pipe large rosettes of whipped cream over the entire surface of the pie. Sprinkle with the grated chocolate just before serving; if desired, garnish each portion with additional banana slices.

Easy Time-Saving and Do-Ahead Tips

SATURDAY

🍃 *Prepare the cream pie to the point of refrigeration. Prepare the onions and bacon for the gravy. Dice the ham and chop the green onions for the greens. Grate the cheese for the macaroni. Bake the sweet potatoes; peel, mash, and refrigerate in a well-sealed container.*

SUNDAY MORNING

🍃 *Prepare the sweet potato casserole to the point of baking. Finish the pie with the whipped cream and shaved chocolate and refrigerate.*

ONE HOUR BEFORE DINNER

🍃 *Bake the sweet potato casserole. Bread and fry the pork chops. Prepare the macaroni.*

Chapter 6

SATISFYING SOUP SUPPERS

TOMATO-RED PEPPER BISQUE

SCALLOP *and* CORN CHOWDER

HEARTY BEEF *and* BARLEY SOUP

APPLE BUTTERNUT SQUASH SOUP

When is dinner supper, and when is supper dinner? It depends on where you're from, and it depends on the time of day. Once, when we were a more agricultural society, farm families came in from the fields and ate a big hot and hearty noontime meal—what those of German heritage call *mittag essen*. In most parts of the country this midday meal was and still is called dinner. Supper was an evening meal and often lighter. Traditionally, Sunday dinner has been a midday meal, just as Christmas day, Easter, and Thanksgiving are midday meals for so many American families. But we often get hungry later in the evening—thus, suppertime.

Hosting a soup supper is such a wonderful and invitingly casual way to gather with our immediate family and friends for a game day, but it is also a wonderful way to meet and greet those in our communities—a casual meal to invite neighbors and meet new friends where the informality is inviting.

For a large group, a soup supper can be an even more wonderful option versus hosting or organizing a big complicated meal. With soup everyone can bring a different family favorite recipe to share; add a salad or two, bake some bread, bring a simple dessert or fresh fruit, and off we go. After all, Sunday dinner is about relationships as much as it is about the foods we enjoy.

Soup suppers are a long-held tradition for many a parish or congregation during Lent. During community service days—where we package boxes for our military men and women serving overseas, make quilts or dresses for those living in poverty, or head out into the local community as a group to serve the needy, the elderly, and shut-ins—a soup supper offers the perfect respite.

No matter what the situation, who doesn't love a good hearty soup? A good soup, a great soup, should taste of the ingredients from which it is made. A great bowl of soup should be satisfying and savory but with a subtle full-bodied flavor that is not overpowered by over seasoning.

Here are four favorites of mine—each one different, each one satisfying, each one inviting and hearty. So call your friends, invite the neighbors, and reach out to those around you—soup and Sundays bring hungry hearts together!

TOMATO-RED PEPPER BISQUE

6 Servings ■ ▪ ▪ ■ ▪ ■ ▪ ■ ▪ ▪ ■ ▪ ■ ▪ ■ ■ ▪ ■ ▪ ■

I love tomato soup and I love the flavor of roasted peppers. Naturally, a combination of the two makes an exceptional pairing. I like to serve this soup with a dollop of sour cream and garnished with fresh basil or dill.

6 large ripe juicy tomatoes, peeled or 1 (28-ounce) can whole peeled tomatoes

2 tablespoons unsalted butter

4 cloves garlic, thinly sliced

1/2 cup diced sweet onions

4 red peppers, roasted and peeled

1 tablespoon all-purpose flour

2 cups chicken broth

1 tablespoon tomato paste

1/2 cup half-and-half

Salt and pepper to season

First, quarter and seed the tomatoes, if using fresh.

Second, heat the butter in a heavy-bottomed pot over medium heat. Add the cloves of garlic and the onion. Cover the skillet and sweat until the garlic and onion are translucent, 2 to 3 minutes. Add the tomatoes and roasted peppers, cover, and sweat for 2 to 3 minutes more. Whisk the flour into the butter and juices, and cook for 2 minutes until a roux forms. Add in the chicken broth and stir until the broth and roux are fully incorporated. Whisk in the tomato paste and simmer until the tomatoes and peppers are fully cooked and beginning to break apart, about 15 minutes.

Third, remove the pot from the heat. Heat the half-and-half in a separate saucepan and bring to a simmer. In a food processor fitted with a steel blade, or with an immersion blender, pulse the tomato and peppers just enough to blend to a soup consistency (do not puree completely or the soup will lose its bright red color). Pour in the hot half-and-half and pulse to blend. Adjust the seasoning to taste.

SCALLOP *and* CORN CHOWDER

6 Servings

Chowder was an early French offering to American cooking. The rich, thick seafood stew is mother to the now-famous soups enjoyed throughout New England. I prepared a variety of chowders at Blair House, including this one, which I served to French President Jacque Chirac.

4 ears sweet corn, shucked

2 cups half-and-half

1/4 cup (1/2 stick) butter, divided

1/2 cup diced celery

2 cloves garlic, minced

1 cup sliced leeks

1/2 cup diced onion

1 pound bay scallops

1 teaspoon fresh thyme leaves

1/4 cup all-purpose flour

4 cups fish stock or clam juice

Salt and white pepper to taste

First, cut the kernels from the cobs with a sharp knife. Reserve the kernels and the cobs.

Second, heat the half-and-half in a medium saucepan until it just begins to boil. Reduce the heat to low, add the cobs, and steep for about 20 minutes. Remove and discard the cobs. Keep the half-and-half warm.

Third, melt 2 tablespoons of the butter in a 2 1/2-quart heavy-bottomed saucepan over medium-low heat. Add in the corn kernels, celery, garlic, leeks, and onion, and sauté for 1 minute. Cover the pan with a tight-fitting lid and allow the vegetables to steam until they are tender and translucent, 2 to 3 minutes.

Fourth, push the vegetables to the sides of the pan. Add the remaining 2 tablespoons of butter into the center of the pan. When the butter begins to bubble, add the scallops and thyme leaves. Cook for 1 to 2 minutes, until the scallops are opaque. Then gently stir together with the vegetables.

Fifth, increase the heat to medium and sprinkle in the flour. Stir the flour into the butter and juices to form a light roux. Pour in the fish stock or clam juice and stir until the mixture is smooth, thick, and bubbly, about 1 minute. Slowly stir in the reserved half-and-half and cook for 3 to 4 minutes more. Season to taste with salt and white pepper.

HEARTY BEEF *and* BARLEY SOUP

This hearty soup with its meaty flavor and nutty barley makes a satisfying simple meal or a great first course—especially on a cold winter day.

1 pound lean beef top round, cut into cubes

1 teaspoon vegetable oil

Salt and cracked black pepper

6 cups beef broth

1 cup diced carrots

1 cup diced celery

2 leeks, white part only, sliced

1 cup diced onions

1 bay leaf

1 sprig thyme

1 cup pearl barley

1 (15-ounce) can home-style stewed tomatoes

1 teaspoon Worcestershire sauce

Salt and pepper to taste

First, in a heavy 2½-quart soup pot, brown the cubed beef in the vegetable oil. Season the beef with a pinch of salt and pepper. Pour in the beef broth and bring to a boil. Reduce the heat to a simmer, and with a ladle skim off any sediment that comes to the surface. Simmer for 40 minutes, until the meat is becoming tender.

Second, add in the carrots, celery, leeks, onions, bay leaf, and thyme. Simmer for 10 minutes. Add in the barley, and simmer for 35 minutes more or until all the vegetables are cooked and the barley is fully cooked but still firm.

Third, when the soup is finished cooking, add the tomatoes with the juice and simmer for 1 minute more. Add the Worcestershire and adjust the seasoning to taste with salt and pepper.

APPLE BUTTERNUT SQUASH SOUP

8 Servings

The combination of sweet cider, crisp apples, earthy sage, and roasted squash is bound to create a memorable, savory soup. Squash is one of the many dishes the American Indians introduced to European settlers and has long been an autumn favorite. I love the nutty aroma that is brought out when squash is roasted.

1 medium butternut squash

Vegetable oil

2 Granny Smith apples, cored and diced

2 carrots, peeled and chopped

1 medium sweet onion, chopped

2 cups apple cider

¼ cup packed light brown sugar

¼ teaspoon ground ginger

½ teaspoon ground allspice

1 sprig fresh sage

4 cups vegetable broth

Salt and white pepper to taste

Oven temperature 350°F.

Roast the squash: First, use a sharp knife to cut the squash in half lengthwise. Remove the seeds and thoroughly clean out any membrane. Rub each half with a little vegetable oil.

Second, place the squash cut side down in an ovenproof baking dish. Bake until the squash is becoming tender, about 40 minutes. Remove from the oven. When cool enough to handle, scoop the flesh into a bowl.

Make the soup: First, combine the apples, carrots, onion, cider, brown sugar, ginger, allspice, and sage in a heavy-bottomed saucepan. Bring to a boil over medium heat, and then reduce to medium-low. Simmer until the carrots are fully cooked, about 25 minutes.

Second, combine the apple mixture with the baked squash. Add in the vegetable broth and heat just until the soup begins to boil. Puree the soup using a counter top or immersion blender . Season to taste with salt and white pepper.

Chapter 7

IN THE GARDEN

MARINATED ARTICHOKE *and* FENNEL SALAD

ONION FOCACCIA

PEPPERONATA

BAKED SEMOLINA GNOCCHI

CANNELLINI BEANS *and* BROCCOLI RABE

CHOCOLATE APRICOT
RICOTTA CHEESECAKE

Call it al fresco, call it dinner in the shade, call it a garden party, leisure dining, or a backyard picnic—eating with friends in the open air on a warm, breezy afternoon and on into the cool of evening is an exceptional pleasure.

There is something about a garden—picturesque and serene, a momentary reflection mirroring nature as it was meant to be and redeeming one small part of the Earth to its intended glory. In the garden it is easy to imagine ourselves in a more leisurely time—eating al fresco is as old as civilization and captured in the mosaics of ancient Greece and Rome. Whether we live along the sun-drenched California coast, the green woods of the Pacific Northwest, in the rolling Heartland hills, lakeside in New England, or along the southern coastal plains, relaxing and laughing in animated conversation beneath the shade trees is quite the place to be.

Sunday dinner in the garden can be casual and unpretentious—fun with a bit of whimsy—where we can relax and the kids can run around. In the garden, we also find the most charming place for special events like a bridal shower, an engagement party, anniversary, or even a wedding—each one a time-honored moment shared with special friends and those we love. Indeed, in the garden we find that perfect place of leisure and an atmosphere of elegance and grace to match that day of celebration and make any occasion one long remembered.

Having a festive Sunday dinner outdoors is not complicated, but it does take some planning. I always begin with foods served cool or cold so everyone can sit down without the host (or chef) worrying about the food getting cold. I then choose main-course dishes that require little last-minute fuss in the kitchen so the hosts can be part of the fest rather than stuck behind the stove. For dessert, something make-ahead and easily served without toppings like whipped cream.

So when the sun dips down behind the mountains or slowly slides into the ocean, when the long rays quietly vanish into cooling shadow amid the vines and orchards, head out into the garden. Here's a menu that calls us to do just that: a menu replete with all the bountiful variety a garden should offer—hearty robust flavors inspired by and found throughout the Mediterranean region and along the California coast.

MARINATED ARTICHOKE
and FENNEL SALAD

8 Servings　■■■■■■■■■■■■■■■■■■■■■■■■■■

In most Mediterranean cultures, vegetables are an integral part of every meal—a tradition that works especially well in California, with its warm climate and incredible produce. Castroville hails as the artichoke capital of the world, which may explain the many wonderful artichoke recipes found in California's Italian-inspired cooking.

ARTICHOKES

4 fresh artichokes

1 lemon, quartered

2 whole cloves garlic

2 tablespoons olive oil, as needed

FENNEL SALAD

4 bulbs fresh fennel

1/4 cup extra-virgin olive oil

Juice of 1 lemon

Salt and pepper to taste

2 tablespoons balsamic vinegar

Prepare the artichokes: First, snap off all the tough outer leaves of the artichokes, and then with a serrated knife cut off the top third of each trimmed artichoke. Use a sharp paring knife to peel away the tough dark-green area around the base of each artichoke, and trim the stems to 1 inch. Quarter each artichoke and cut away the fuzzy interior. Rub the quartered artichokes with two of the lemon quarters to prevent discoloration. Reserve the used lemon quarters for cooking the artichokes.

Second, place the artichokes, along with the two squeezed lemon quarters, the garlic, and a splash of olive oil, into a skillet. Add enough cold salted water to cover them completely. Bring to a boil over medium heat, then cover with a tight-fitting lid and cook the artichokes until tender, approximately 20 minutes. Drain the artichokes, transfer to a stainless bowl, squeeze the juice from the remaining 2 lemon quarters over them and drizzle with a little olive oil. Set aside.

Prepare the fennel: Cut the long, fernlike stalks off the fennel bulbs, reserving a few of the sprigs. Trim away any outer bottom leaves that are discolored. Cut the bulbs in half lengthwise, then lay each half flat on a clean cutting board and finely shred into thin slices with a sharp kitchen knife. Finely chop 1 tablespoon of the reserved fennel fronds and toss together with the shredded bulbs in a stainless bowl, along with the extra-virgin olive oil and lemon juice. Season to taste with salt and pepper.

Assemble the salad: Mound the marinated fennel in the center of a platter and arrange the artichokes around the outside. Drizzle the salad with a little more extra-virgin olive oil and the balsamic vinegar.

ONION FOCACCIA

These flat rustic loaves are a favorite throughout Italy and in California, where they most likely arrived with families from Liguria. Focaccia in Liguria is topped with onions and enjoyed primarily as a snack. It is the perfect accompaniment to the pepperonata or for sopping up the olive oil–balsamic dressing in the fennel and artichoke salad.

FOCACCIA

I package (I 1/2 teaspoons) active dry yeast

1/4 cup warm water, about 110°F

I 1/2 cups water, room temperature

2 tablespoons olive oil

3 1/2 cups bread flour, divided

I teaspoon coarse salt

TOPPING

2 teaspoons olive oil

2 cups thinly sliced onion

Olive oil for brushing

Pinch of coarse salt

Oven temperature 400°F.

Make the focaccia dough: First, sprinkle the yeast over the warm water and let the mixture stand for 1 minute, then stir until the yeast is dissolved.

Second, combine the olive oil with 1 1/2 cups water in a mixing bowl and blend in the dissolved yeast. Use a wooden spoon to add in 2 cups of the bread flour; stir until the mixture reaches the consistency of thick batter. Continue stirring until the dough is smooth and elastic, about 200 strokes. Scrape down the sides of the bowl with a rubber spatula, cover with a clean tea towel, and set in a draft-free place until the dough is bubbly and has doubled in volume, about 1 hour.

Third, whisk the remaining bread flour together with the salt in a separate bowl. Place the bubbly dough in an electric mixer fitted with a dough hook and add in the flour mixture on low speed, 1/2 cup at a time. The dough should be sticking just a little to the sides of the bowl. Add in additional flour if necessary, and knead on low

speed for about 10 minutes. Transfer the dough to a clean, lightly oiled bowl; cover with a clean tea towel and set in a draft-free place until it has again doubled in volume, about 1 hour.

Prepare the topping: Heat 2 teaspoons of olive oil in a skillet over medium heat. Add in the sliced onion and sauté just long enough to soften, about 1 minute. Set aside to cool.

Assemble the focaccia: First, shape the dough by gently pulling it, starting from the middle, until it forms a 12 x 18-inch rectangle. Transfer it to a lightly oiled baking sheet, and use two fingers to make little indentations over the entire surface. Lightly brush the dough with lukewarm water, and let it rise uncovered for 30 minutes.

Second, carefully brush the focaccia with a little olive oil; sprinkle the surface evenly with the sautéed onions, and season with a pinch of coarse salt. Bake the focaccia on the top oven rack until crusty and brown, 20 to 25 minutes.

PEPPERONATA

8 Servings ▪ ▪▪ ▪ ▪ ▪▪ ▪

Pepperonata is a slow-simmered dish made with peppers and tomatoes and seasoned with either basil or Italian parsley; it can also include carrots, zucchini, and olives. This particular variation, prepared with roasted peppers, is really quite wonderful served as a starter with the baked focaccia.

2 red bell peppers

2 yellow bell peppers

1/2 cup olive oil

2 cloves garlic, thinly sliced

1 small onion, quartered and separated

6 large plum tomatoes, peeled and seeded, or 1 (24-ounce) can Italian plum tomatoes

1/4 cup dry white wine

2 teaspoons chopped fresh Italian parsley

Salt and pepper to taste

First, brush the outside of each pepper lightly with a little olive oil. Using tongs to turn them, grill the peppers directly over a gas flame for about 10 minutes. Or place them on a baking sheet and broil 3 inches under the heat, using tongs to turn them, for approximately 10 minutes. When they are done, the skins of the peppers should be completely charred and blistered. Transfer them to a sealed plastic bag and let them steam for 10 minutes. When the peppers are cool enough to handle, peel the charred skin and remove the stems and seeds, and quarter each pepper lengthwise.

Second, heat the olive oil over medium heat in an 8-inch oval casserole, and sauté the garlic and onion until translucent, 2 to 3 minutes.

Third, cut the tomatoes into large chunks. Toss the peppers and tomatoes with the sautéed garlic and onion in the oval casserole. Add the dry white wine and let simmer for 2 to 3 minutes. Stir in the Italian parsley, then season to taste with salt and pepper. Drizzle a little extra olive oil over the top and simmer, covered, over low heat for 20 minutes. Serve cooled to room temperature.

BAKED SEMOLINA GNOCCHI

8 Servings

Gnocchi, which are little dumplings, can be made a variety of ways. Some recipes use mashed potatoes, others cornmeal, or ricotta cheese and spinach. Gnocchi might be dropped into boiling water, sautéed in hot oil, or—like these—cut into shapes and baked. These gnocchi are also wonderful poached in boiling water and smothered in a tomato or Bolognese sauce.

4 cups whole milk

¹/2 teaspoon salt

I ¹/2 cups fine semolina

¹/2 cup (I stick) butter, divided

I ¹/2 cups coarsely grated Parmesan cheese

2 large egg yolks, room temperature

Oven temperature 400°F.

First, bring the milk to a rolling boil over medium-high heat in a heavy-bottomed saucepan. Add in the salt and then, stirring constantly with a wooden spoon, slowly add in the semolina. Reduce the heat to low, and stir until the mixture is thick and smooth, about 10 minutes. Remove the pan from the heat, and beat in 6 tablespoons of the butter and all of the Parmesan cheese. Allow the mixture to cool slightly, and then beat in the egg yolks.

Second, spread the mixture into a lightly oiled glass dish or casserole; brush the top lightly with oil and cool to room temperature. Refrigerate for at least 2 hours.

Third, melt 2 tablespoons of butter. Scoop out rounded oval portions of the chilled gnocchi dough, each about 2 tablespoons in volume. Gently form the dough into egg-shaped dumplings about 1³/4 inches in length. Layer the gnocchi in alternating circles in the bottom of a lightly oiled casserole, brushing melted butter over each layer.

Fourth, mound the gnocchi layer by layer like a small pyramid. Bake uncovered until golden, about 20 minutes.

CANNELLINI BEANS *and* BROCCOLI RAAB

8 Servings

Broccoli raab or rapini (brassica rapa) is a leafy green and member of the mustard family. The tender stalks and small buds are similar to brocolinni. I like to serve them on their own with just a touch of garlic and extra-virgin olive oil. But I think you'll find that the contrasting textures of the beans and leafy greens create a wonderful combination and exceptional flavor balance.

CANNELLINI BEANS

I cup dried cannellini beans

2 cups chicken broth

1/2 cup diced celery

1/2 cup diced onion

I bay leaf

2 whole cloves garlic

I teaspoon salt

BROCCOLI RAAB

2 bunches fresh broccoli raab

1/4 cup olive oil

2 ounces pancetta, cut into lardons

4 cloves garlic, thinly sliced

Salt to taste

1/4 teaspoon crushed red pepper

Prepare the beans: First, pick through the beans and rinse them thoroughly. Soak the beans for 8 hours or overnight in 1 quart of cold water; then drain.

Second, return the soaked beans to the pot. Pour in the chicken broth, and fill the pot with enough fresh water to cover the beans. Add the celery, onion, bay leaf, and garlic to the pot. Bring to a boil and then reduce the heat and simmer, covered, until the beans are tender, approximately 1 hour.

Prepare the broccoli raab: First, cut any woody ends from the raab and drop the stalks into a shallow pan filled with boiling salted water. Allow the raab to cook for 2 to 3 minutes, then immediately plunge into a bowl of ice water to stop the cooking process. Drain after 2 minutes and cut the leafy green into large pieces.

Prepare the dish: First, heat the olive oil in a skillet over medium heat. Add in the pancetta, stirring from time to time, until it is beginning to brown, 3 to 4 minutes. Add in the sliced garlic, and cook for 1 minute more.

Second, increase the heat to high. Add in the blanched broccoli raab and toss well in the oil for 1 minute. Season with salt and the crushed red pepper flakes. Add 1/2 cup of the bean liquid, cover with a tight-fitting lid and steam for 3 to 4 minutes.

To serve: Toss the beans in with the broccoli raab, along with enough of the cooking liquid so that the dish is moist. Place the beans and raab on a platter and drizzle with a little extra-virgin olive oil.

CHOCOLATE APRICOT RICOTTA CHEESECAKE

10 Servings

During the early 1970s, my mother was the business manager for one of the finest restaurants in Beverly Hills, which specialized in French and Italian cuisine. As I was beginning my career, I'd moonlight there on busy weekends just to gain experience. Some of the truly splendid desserts served at that restaurant included crepes, tiramisu, and zabaglione. I was intrigued by what the pastry chef often boxed up for his family's Sunday dinner: a rustic ricotta cheesecake, like this one, chock-full of bittersweet chocolate and candied fruit.

BISCOTTI CRUST

1 (8-ounce) package almond biscotti

1/4 cup (1/2 stick) butter, melted

CHEESECAKE FILLING

2 teaspoons orange zest

4 ounces bittersweet chocolate

3 ounces dried apricots

1 (4-ounce) package Italian Amaretti cookies, crushed

1 (8-ounce) package cream cheese

1 cup granulated sugar

1/2 teaspoon salt

1/2 tablespoon pure almond extract

2 pounds whole-milk ricotta cheese

6 large eggs, room temperature

1/2 cup all-purpose flour

FRUIT TOPPING

8 medium ripe apricots

4 ripe nectarines

2 tablespoons sugar

2 tablespoons Amaretto or almond syrup

Oven temperature 300°F.

Prepare the crust: Break the biscotti into small pieces. Place the crushed biscotti in the bowl of a food processor fitted with a steel blade; pulse to make fine crumbs. Pour in the melted butter and pulse until well blended. Press the crust into the bottom and about 1 inch up the sides of a 9-inch springform pan.

Prepare the filling: First, pour in just enough water to cover the orange zest and heat in a small pan for 2 to 3 minutes or in a small dish of water in the microwave for 1 to 2 minutes; this process will extract the bitter oil. Drain the zest thoroughly and set aside.

Second, chop the chocolate into pieces about half the size of chocolate chips and set aside. Dice the apricots into small pieces (you should end up with about 2/3 cup) and set aside. Place the biscotti in a sealable plastic bag and gently crush with a rolling pin (you should end up with about 1 cup of tiny pieces); set aside.

Third, combine the cream cheese and sugar in the bowl of a mixer fitted with a paddle and beat on medium speed until there are no lumps.

Fourth, turn the mixer speed to low, add in the salt and almond extract and beat for 1 minute. Turn the machine off and scrape down the sides of the bowl with a rubber spatula.

Fifth, return the mixer speed to low and add in the ricotta, a cup at a time, until fully blended and smooth. Add in the eggs one at a time, allowing each egg to blend into the cheese mixture before adding the next. Then add in the flour, a tablespoon at a time, and mix just long enough to fully incorporate all the ingredients. (Note: It is important that you don't overmix the filling when making a cheesecake; air beaten into the batter will cause the cake to crack when it is baked.)

Sixth, use a rubber spatula to fold the orange zest, chopped chocolate, and apricots into the ricotta mixture; then fold in the crushed biscotti. Pour the filling into the prepared crust. Smooth the top and lightly tap the sides of the pan to knock out any air bubbles.

Bake the cheesecake: First, bake the cheesecake on a baking sheet in the center of the oven for 50 minutes; this will allow the thick center of the cake to rise evenly to temperature. Increase the oven temperature to 350°F and continue baking for another 25 to 30 minutes. The cheesecake is completely baked when the edges begin to brown and rise slightly above the center. The center will still jiggle slightly, like custard.

Second, turn off the oven, set the oven door ajar and allow the cheesecake to cool for 30 minutes undisturbed; this will keep the center from falling.

Third, transfer the cheesecake to a cooling rack and carefully run a thin knife about 1 inch deep around the inside rim of the pan. (As the cheesecake cools, it will pull into the center; loosening the cake from the edges of the pan will reduce the chance of cracks forming on the surface.) Cool to room temperature in the pan, then cover tightly with plastic wrap and refrigerate for at least 4 hours and up to 2 days.

Prepare the topping: Cut the apricots into quarters and slice the nectarines. Toss them together in a stainless or glass bowl with the sugar and Amaretto or almond syrup. Allow the fruit to macerate for 1 hour before service.

To serve: Run a thin knife around the inside edge of the cake pan, and then carefully loosen the spring and remove the ring. Transfer the cheesecake to a decorative cake stand. (Note: It is helpful to cut each slice of cheesecake with a thin sharp knife that has been dipped in warm water.) Serve topped with the apricots and nectarines.

Easy Time-Saving and Do-Ahead Tips

SATURDAY:

- Prepare the gnocchi dough and refrigerate.
- Bake the cheesecake and refrigerate.
- Prepare the artichokes and refrigerate in a stainless bowl.
- Prepare the vegetables for the pepperonata and refrigerate in well-sealed containers.
- Soak the beans.

TWO HOURS BEFORE DINNER:

- Prepare the roast for the oven.
- Bake the focaccia.
- Prepare the gnocchi for the oven.
- Prepare the apricots and nectarines.

Chapter 8

A SUNDAY *for* THANKSGIVING

SAVORY TURKEY *and* VEGETABLE POT PIE

SWEET POTATO BISCUITS

MOLDED CRANBERRY, APPLE,
and ORANGE RING

SPICED PUMPKIN MOUSSE CAKE

Throughout history and around the world, harvest festivals have been held to celebrate the gathering of the year's crops. In 1621, however, when the Pilgrims invited their Indian neighbors to a dinner in honor of their first harvest, a distinctly American tradition was born. Today, we are one of a few nations to observe an official day of thanksgiving.

Thanksgiving has always been more than just a harvest festival. It has also been a time to refocus our attention—to acknowledge God's "manifold blessings" and the earth's plentiful abundance. George Washington was the first president to proclaim a national day of thanksgiving. Later, during the Civil War, President Lincoln set aside the last Thursday of November "as a day of Thanksgiving and Praise to our beneficent Father." After that it became a tradition for each president to proclaim an annual day of thanks. This continued until 1941, when Congress finally established Thanksgiving Day as a national holiday.

And so, on the fourth Thursday of November, Americans of all backgrounds gather to give thanks with a feast of traditional foods harvested from our land: turkey, corn, squash, pumpkin, sweet potatoes, and cranberries. How each family prepares those traditional ingredients and what unique cooking styles are incorporated into this singular meal is as diverse as our citizenry.

Thanksgiving has always been one of my favorite holidays. Like most Americans I have fond memories of my family's celebration. Each year our family gathers to share a traditional meal complete with hearty seafood chowder, juicy herb-scented roasted turkey, savory cornbread dressing, sparkling cider, and rich homey desserts. This is a joyous time to remember our heritage, our family, and all the blessings we have enjoyed throughout the year. Every year, however, we seem to face the same universal challenges: How do we fit all those leftovers into the crowded refrigerator? What do we do with that picked-over turkey carcass?

My wife and I met these challenges years ago when we began the tradition of making turkey pot pie from our leftover bird and serving it the Sunday following Thanksgiving. We've come to anticipate this savory and satisfying entrée as much as the Thanksgiving dinner itself. It is a perfect Sunday dinner: very easy, mostly prepared ahead, and memorably delicious. I think you'll agree that leftovers never tasted better! Of course, you don't have to wait until November. After all, Sunday dinner should be like having Thanksgiving every week.

SAVORY TURKEY *and* VEGETABLE POT PIE

8 Servings ■

Creating this excellent pot pie couldn't be easier. One way to save on time is by making a little extra crust when you prepare your Thanksgiving pies. Then, when those dinner dishes are being scraped and stacked, take a few moments to prepare a rich stock from the turkey carcass and a few of the vegetables and herbs you'll no doubt have on hand. Trust me: As you organize things to prepare the stock, a lot of that leftover Thanksgiving mess on the stovetop will disappear in the process.

TURKEY STOCK

1 whole turkey carcass

8 cups cold water

1 carrot, peeled and chopped

2 ribs celery, chopped

1 leek, white part only, thinly sliced

1 medium onion, diced

1 whole clove garlic

1 bay leaf

1 small bouquet of fresh herbs:
parsley, rosemary, sage, and thyme

6 to 8 white peppercorns

2 chicken bouillon cubes or 2
tablespoons concentrated chicken
stock

PASTRY DOUGH

3 cups all-purpose flour

1 teaspoon salt

1/2 cup (1 stick) unsalted butter

1/2 cup shortening

4 to 5 tablespoons cold milk

POT PIE FILLING

1/2 cup (1 stick) butter

1/2 cup diced celery

2 cloves garlic, minced

1/2 cup diced onion

1 cup peeled sliced carrots

1 cup peeled pearl onions

6 tablespoons all-purpose flour

4 cups turkey stock

Salt and white pepper to taste

4 cups roasted turkey, cubed

1 cup cooked or frozen peas, thawed

1 tablespoon fresh chopped herbs:
parsley, rosemary, sage, and thyme

Prepare the stock: First, cut away the extra meat from the turkey breast and remove the legs and thighs. Trim the remaining meat from the legs and thighs, keeping the larger pieces for sandwiches or other favorites, and set aside about 4 cups of the smaller pieces, as well as any little bits of extra white and dark meat, for the pie filling. Scrape any lingering dressing from the carcass, but don't worry if a little remains—the flavor will only enhance the pie. Use a pair of poultry shears to carefully cut through the breastbone and back.

Second, place the turkey carcass, as well as the leg, thigh, and wing bones, into a large pot and pour in the 8 cups cold water. Add the chopped carrot, celery, leek, onion, garlic, bay leaf, bouquet of fresh herbs, white peppercorns, and bouillon cubes.

Third, heat the stock until the water just begins to boil. Reduce the heat and simmer uncovered until the liquid is reduced by half, about 3 hours. This should yield about 4 cups of stock. Cool slightly, discard the turkey bones, and strain through a fine sieve. Cool the stock to room temperature and refrigerate in a well-sealed container for up to a week.

Prepare the pastry dough: First, whisk the flour and salt together using a stiff wire whisk. Cut in the butter and shortening with a pastry cutter, or pulse for several seconds in a food processor, until the mixture reaches the consistency of coarse crumbly meal.

Second, add the milk one tablespoon at a time and toss together with a fork. If using a food processor pulse a second or two until the liquid is incorporated and the moistened dough is just beginning to come together. Remove the mixture from the bowl or food processor, turn out onto a clean dry surface and knead the dough just enough to form a pliable, tender ball. Divide into two portions and roll into balls. Flatten each ball into a disk by gently pressing it between your hands.

Third, wrap the disks in plastic wrap and chill for at least 30 minutes. The dough may be kept in the refrigerator, wrapped tightly, for up to a week.

Prepare the filling: First, melt the butter in a skillet over medium heat. Add in the celery, garlic, and onion, and sauté until the onion becomes translucent, 2 to 3 minutes. Regulate the heat carefully to ensure that the butter doesn't brown. Add the carrots and pearl onions, and sauté for 2 more minutes. Sprinkle the flour over the sautéed vegetables and stir until the flour combines with the butter to form a roux.

Second, pour in the stock, stirring constantly to keep lumps from forming, and simmer until the sauce has thickened to the desired consistency, 3 to 4 minutes. Season to taste with the salt and white pepper and remove the pan from the stove. Fold in the cubed turkey meat, peas, and fresh herbs and cool the mixture to room temperature. This filling may be used right away or refrigerated in a well-sealed container for up to 4 days.

Assemble the turkey pot pie: First, lightly dust a rolling pin and a clean work surface with a little flour, and then roll out one of the chilled pastry disks into a circle that is about 1/4-inch thick and about 12 inches in diameter. Carefully drape the pastry over the rolling pin and transfer it to a 10-inch deep-dish pie pan.

Second, spoon the filling into the dish. Roll out the second piece of dough so that it is slightly smaller in diameter and just a bit thicker than the bottom crust, and carefully place it over the filling. Use a sharp knife or kitchen shears to trim away any excess dough, and then crimp the edges. Cut several slits into the top of the crust and brush with a little milk. (Extra pieces of dough can be cut into attractive shapes and arranged decoratively over the surface of the pie.)

Third, bake in a 350°F oven until the crust is golden and the filling is bubbling hot, 60 to 70 minutes. Remove the pot pie from the oven and let it rest at room temperature for 20 minutes before serving.

SWEET POTATO BISCUITS

18 Biscuits ■ ▪ ■ ▪ ■ ▪ ■ ▪ ■ ▪ ■ ▪ ■ ▪ ■ ▪ ■ ▪ ■ ▪ ■ ▪ ■ ▪ ■

These biscuits are especially good served hot and oozing with creamy maple–walnut butter.

2 $^1/_2$ **cups all-purpose flour**

2 **tablespoons baking powder**

Pinch of allspice

Pinch of ground cloves

$^1/_2$ **teaspoon salt**

$^1/_4$ **cup packed light brown sugar**

$^1/_4$ **cup ($^1/_2$ stick) unsalted butter, chilled**

$^1/_2$ **cup shortening, chilled**

1 $^1/_2$ **cups mashed sweet potatoes or yams**

Oven temperature 400°F.

First, sift the flour, baking powder, allspice, ground cloves, and salt into a large bowl. Use the tips of your fingers to blend in the brown sugar.

Second, cut in the chilled butter and shortening with a pastry cutter or pulse in a food processor until the mixture resembles coarse crumbly meal. Then stir in the mashed sweet potatoes and knead until the dough just holds together.

Third, turn the dough out onto a lightly floured surface. Knead gently for 1 minute, adding a little extra flour as necessary, to incorporate all the ingredients and ensure that the biscuits will rise evenly. Pat the dough into a $^1/_2$-inch-thick circle and let it rest, covered with a clean tea towel, for 10 to 15 minutes.

Fourth, cut out the biscuits with a 2-inch round cutter dipped in flour. Gather the scraps, pat out again, and cut into biscuits. Arrange them about $^3/_4$-inch apart on an ungreased baking sheet and brush the tops with a little milk.

Fifth, bake the biscuits until golden brown, 10 to 12 minutes. Cool the biscuits on racks and brush with a little melted butter.

MOLDED CRANBERRY, APPLE, *and* ORANGE RING

8 to 10 Servings ▪▪▪▪▪▪▪▪▪▪▪▪▪▪▪▪▪▪▪▪▪▪

The tang of cranberries and orange with crunchy apples makes a festive salad—leftover cranberry sauce never had it so good!

2 oranges, peels on, seeded and cut into chunks

1 (12-ounce) package fresh cranberries

1 1/2 cups granulated sugar

2 tablespoons unflavored gelatin

2 cups cranberry-apple juice cocktail

2 cups whole-cranberry sauce

2 cups diced red or green apples

First, combine the orange chunks with the fresh cranberries and 1/2 cup of the sugar in the bowl of a food processor fitted with a steel blade. Roughly chop by pulsing for 5 to 10 seconds. Set aside.

Second, sprinkle the gelatin and the remaining 1 cup of sugar into the cranberry-apple juice in a small saucepan. Bring the mixture to a boil over medium heat and stir until the sugar and gelatin are completely dissolved, about 5 minutes.

Third, combine the hot cranberry-apple juice mixture and the whole-berry cranberry sauce in a stainless bowl. Stir together well, let stand for 5 minutes, and then partially submerge in a bowl of ice water. Stir until cool. When the mixture has cooled completely, fold in the diced apples and the chopped orange-cranberry mixture.

Fourth, pour into a 2-quart mold and refrigerate, covered, until the salad is set, at least 8 hours or overnight. Serve if desired, garnished with fresh orange slices and sugar-frosted cranberries.

SPICED PUMPKIN MOUSSE CAKE

12 Servings ▮▮▮▮▮▮▮▮▮▮▮▮▮▮▮▮▮▮▮▮▮▮▮▮▮▮▮▮

There always seems to be at least one unused can of pumpkin left in the cupboard after Thanksgiving (you'll need a 29-ounce can for this recipe). If your home is anything like ours, you'll no doubt have plenty of leftover whipped cream on hand, as well. This amazing cake is rich, creamy, light, and airy—and the combination of spices creates a fabulous dessert.

PUMPKIN CAKE

1 cup all-purpose flour

3/4 teaspoon baking soda

1/4 teaspoon ground allspice

1/2 teaspoon ground cinnamon

1/4 teaspoon ground nutmeg

1/4 teaspoon salt

1/2 cup (1 stick) unsalted butter

1/2 cup granulated sugar

1/2 cup packed dark brown sugar

1 large egg, room temperature

1 1/3 cups canned pumpkin

1/2 cup dark raisins

MOUSSE FILLING

2 cups half-and-half

1/3 cup brandy or 1/4 cup water plus
   1 tablespoon brandy flavoring

2 tablespoons unflavored gelatin

4 large egg yolks, room temperature

1 2/3 cups canned pumpkin

3/4 cup granulated sugar

1/2 cup light brown sugar

1 teaspoon ground allspice

1 teaspoon ground cinnamon

1/2 teaspoon ground cloves

2 cups heavy whipping cream

Oven temperature 350°F.

Make the cake: First, lightly grease a 9-inch springform pan.

Second, sift the flour, baking soda, allspice, cinnamon, nutmeg, and salt into a mixing bowl and set aside.

Third, thoroughly cream the butter with the granulated sugar and brown sugar in the bowl of an electric mixer fitted with a paddle until light and fluffy, about 6 minutes. Scrape down the sides of the bowl with a rubber spatula. Then, with the mixer running at medium speed, add in the egg and beat until the egg is fully incorporated into the butter mixture.

Fourth, turn the mixer speed to low and add the sifted dry ingredients in 3 stages alternately with the pumpkin, mixing well after each addition. Increase the mixer speed to medium and beat for about 30 seconds. Then scrape down the sides of the bowl and fold in the raisins.

Fifth, spread the batter evenly in the springform pan. Place the pan on the middle rack of the oven and bake until a wooden pick comes out clean when inserted into the middle, 35 to 40 minutes. (The cake will only rise to a height of approximately 1 inch.) Cool the cake in the pan. When the cake is cool, wipe along the inside edge of the springform pan with a damp paper towel, then lightly butter the clean edge.

Make the mousse: First, scald the half-and-half in a saucepan by heating it just to the point of boiling. Quickly remove the pan from the heat and cool until it is lukewarm.

Second, pour the brandy into a small bowl and sprinkle the gelatin over it. Stir until the gelatin has dissolved.

Third, combine the egg yolks with the pumpkin, granulated sugar, brown sugar, allspice, cinnamon, and cloves in the top of a double boiler or in a stainless bowl. Stir well to incorporate.

Fourth, whip the heavy cream until stiff peaks form. Cover and refrigerate.

Fifth, add the softened gelatin to the scalded half-and-half and stir to dissolve so that there are no lumps, and then slowly pour it into the pumpkin mixture, stirring constantly. Place the bowl over a double boiler or pan of rapidly boiling water—do not allow the pan to touch the water—and stir with a heat-resistant rubber spatula until the pumpkin mousse has thickened slightly and is barely bubbling around the edges, about 5 minutes. Remove the mousse from the pan of boiling water and submerge it partially in a pan of ice water. Cool, stirring constantly, to room temperature. As the custard cools, it will begin to set up and have the consistency of cake batter.

Sixth, just when the custard begins to set up, add half of the stiffly whipped cream to it and stir until fully incorporated; then quickly but gently fold in the remaining whipped cream. Pour the mousse over the cake in the cake pan, tapping the edges of the pan to get rid of any air bubbles. Chill uncovered in the refrigerator until the mousse is completely cool, about 1 hour. Cover tightly with plastic wrap and refrigerate for at least 8 hours or overnight.

To serve: Wrap a warm damp tea towel around the outer rim of the pan for a minute or so, then carefully run a thin sharp knife around the inside of the pan. Loosen the springform ring and transfer the cake to your favorite cake stand. If desired, garnish the cake just before serving with rosettes of whipped cream and lightly dust the top with pumpkin pie spice.

Easy Time-Saving and Do-Ahead Tips

THANKSGIVING NIGHT:

Make the turkey stock.

SATURDAY:

Bake the cake.

Prepare the turkey pot pie filling and the pastry dough; refrigerate separately.

Prepare the mousse and assemble the cake.

Prepare the biscuit dough and the molded salad; seal both in plastic wrap and refrigerate.

SUNDAY MORNING:

Assemble the turkey pot pie.

AN HOUR AND A HALF BEFORE DINNER:

Bake the turkey pot pie.

Cut out the biscuits, to be baked when the turkey pot pie is through cooking.

Chapter 9

DOWN HILL
COUNTRY

CHICKEN FRIED STEAK *with* CREAM GRAVY

GREEN BEANS *with* SMOKED
BACON *and* ONIONS

FLAKY BUTTERMILK BISCUITS

HOMINY SPOON BREAD

MOLASSES-PECAN CAKE *with* CARAMEL
BUTTERCREAM FROSTING

The time was, not so long ago, when most Americans lived on small farms or around the small towns dotted between the railroad lines and winding U.S. highways that once connected so much of the country. Their world centered on the daily chores of rural life. They patterned their own clothes, grew their own vegetables, and raised enough chickens and hogs for their own tables.

Around the bustling town square—with the post office, diner, hardware store, barbershop, and filling station—under the welcome shade of ancient poplars, cottonwoods, and oaks; and up and down quiet streets, neighbors knew neighbors and joined one another for worship on Sunday. Waiting back home was the Sunday table, overflowing with simple, satisfying flavors. The Hill Country of Texas is still such a place.

My wife and I lived in San Antonio, Texas, when our children were young and it's where our youngest was born. We ventured throughout the region in search of great tamales, barbeque brisket, and chicken fried steak. The Hill Country is replete with rolling hills and endless fields of wildflowers—kept green by the rivers and aquifer feed springs around rivers and that's where the cities of Austin, San Marcos, and New Braunfels sprang up. The cultural influences are many, but one may surprise you. Texas has one of our country's largest populations of German heritage. Indeed, much of the local music is a cultural blend, where the accordions of German polka meet the guitar strings of old Mexico.

Chicken fried steak, also known in some regions as country fried steak, has long been a Sunday favorite—especially in the South and out West, where so much beef is raised. But nowhere in the U.S. is chicken fried steak savored with more passion than deep in the heart of Texas. Some folks call this "The National Dish of Texas!" Many Texans down in Hill Country readily credit the creation of chicken fried steak to their German immigrant grandparents—for it is similar in some ways to Wiener Schnitzel. True or not, beef was certainly plentiful in their adopted central Texas home, and an otherwise tough piece of meat could be cut thin, pounded, seasoned well, and fried to become a tender and delicious entrée.

So come on down to Hill Country. Gather a bunch of Bluebonnets from along a country road. Enjoy the buttered hot biscuits, tall cool pitchers of sweetened iced tea, and platters piled high. On the sideboard, a beautiful, mouthwatering cake proudly stands in wait. All bid us home—like the welcome call hollered from the screened front door: "Come on in. Dinner's ready!"

CHICKEN FRIED STEAK
with CREAM GRAVY

8 Servings

The key to good chicken fried steak is a fully tenderized and thinly pounded piece of beef. I prefer bottom round steak, but top round or chuck steak works quite well. The meat should be seasoned before being breaded and then slowly pan fried—never deep fried—in just the minimal amount of shortening needed to cover the breaded steaks halfway and thoroughly fry to a crisp golden crust.

CHICKEN FRIED STEAK

3 pounds bottom round steak, 1/2-inch thick or 8 (6-ounce) cube steaks

I teaspoon granulated garlic

2 teaspoons paprika

I teaspoon ground black pepper

1/8 teaspoon ground red (cayenne) pepper

I teaspoon ground white pepper

2 teaspoons salt

I cup all purpose flour

3 eggs

3/4 cup milk

2 cups breadcrumbs

Vegetable shortening for frying

CREAM GRAVY

4 tablespoons all-purpose flour

3 cups whole milk

2 cups chicken broth

Salt and ground black pepper to taste

Make the chicken fried steak: First, cut the bottom round into eight equal 6-ounce pieces. In a small bowl, combine the granulated garlic, paprika, black pepper, cayenne pepper, white pepper, and salt; mix well.

Second, place the pieces of steak on a clean dry cutting board. Using the spiked side of a meat tenderizer, pound the steaks up and down and across each piece and on both sides to break down the gristly fibers. Place each piece of meat between two pieces of plastic wrap and pound the steaks again, using the flat smooth side of the tenderizer, until the steaks are about 1/4-inch thick. (Skip this process for store-bought cube steaks.)

Third, evenly sprinkle the seasoning on both sides of each steak and rub the seasoning thoroughly into the meat.

Fourth, set up a dredging station. In one dish place the flour. In the second dish beat the eggs together with the milk. In the third dish place the bread crumbs. Dredge the seasoned steaks in the flour, followed by the egg wash and then the breadcrumbs. Press the breadcrumbs firmly onto each steak, and place the breaded steaks on a sheet of parchment or waxed paper.

Fifth, melt enough of the shortening in a skillet so that the breaded steaks will be immersed halfway when fried. Heat the melted shortening over medium-high heat to 325°F or until a pinch of flour sizzles when sprinkled into the oil. Add the steaks and regulate the heat so the steaks fry slowly and evenly. Most likely, you'll do this in two batches. Turn the steaks over when they have begun to brown, after 4 to 5 minutes, and when the meat juices begin to appear in the top of the steaks; fry each steak on the second side for 4 to 5 minutes more.

Sixth, blot the steaks on paper towels, place on a wire rack set in a baking sheet and keep warm in a 250°F oven until service.

Make the cream gravy: Pour off all but 4 tablespoons of the oil in the skillet and return to medium-high heat. Sprinkle the flour over the oil and stir to form a paste. Slowly pour in the milk and chicken broth, whisking constantly and scraping the brown meaty pieces from the bottom of the skillet. Continue whisking until the liquid blends with the flour and oil to form the gravy. Turn the heat to low and let the gravy simmer for a few minutes; just before serving, season to taste with salt and pepper.

To serve: Pour a generous amount of the gravy over each fried steak and pass the extra gravy in a gravy boat.

GREEN BEANS *with* SMOKED BACON *and* ONIONS

8 Servings

My grandmother always cooked her homegrown pole beans with bacon and onions. True to her generation, however, they were usually boiled. I prefer mine sautéed and bright green, with just a little snap left to them.

2 pounds green beans
4 strips thick-cut smoked bacon, diced
1 medium onion, thinly sliced
Pinch of salt

First, use a sharp paring knife to trim the ends and pull any tough strings from the green beans.

Second, blanch the beans in a large saucepan filled with boiling salted water. They should cook just long enough to become tender and turn bright green, about 3 to 4 minutes. Drain the beans and immediately plunge them into ice water to stop the cooking process.

Third, cook the bacon in a large skillet over medium-high heat until it begins to brown, then add the blanched beans and onion slices and season with a pinch of salt. Toss thoroughly with the bacon fat.

Fourth, reduce the heat to medium and sauté until the beans are cooked through and the onions have begun to caramelize, 4 to 5 minutes.

FLAKY BUTTERMILK BISCUITS

18 Biscuits ▪ ▪ ▪ ▪ ▪ ▪ ▪ ▪ ▪ ▪ ▪ ▪ ▪ ▪ ▪

On a nineteenth–century farm you would have churned your own butter and afterward enjoyed a tall glass of cold buttermilk—sweet, creamy, and with bits of butter floating on the surface. Cultured buttermilk is not nearly as good, but it still makes for some of the best, flakiest biscuits ever!

4 cups all-purpose flour

5 teaspoons baking powder

1 teaspoon baking soda

1 teaspoon salt

1 cup shortening, chilled

1 1/2 cups buttermilk

Oven temperature 450°F.

First, sift the flour, baking powder, baking soda, and salt into a large bowl. Cut the chilled shortening into pieces and add to the dry ingredients. Use a pastry cutter to cut in the shortening, or pulse for several seconds in a food processor, until the mixture resembles coarse crumbly meal. Add the buttermilk and stir with a fork until the dough just holds together.

Second, turn the dough out onto a lightly floured surface. Knead gently for 1 minute, adding a little extra flour as necessary to incorporate all the ingredients and ensure that the biscuits will rise evenly. Pat into a 1/2-inch-thick circle and let the dough rest, covered with a clean tea towel, for 10 to 15 minutes.

Third, cut the biscuits with a 2-inch round cutter dipped in flour. Arrange them about 3/4-inch apart on an ungreased baking sheet, and brush the tops with a little buttermilk. Bake until golden, 10 to 12 minutes. Cool the biscuits on wire racks and brush them with melted butter, if desired.

HOMINY SPOON BREAD

8 Servings

Hominy, made from boiled white corn, is a truly American product. In many areas of the country, hominy is served baked in a casserole with squash and cheese. Grits, which are often served for breakfast, are made from ground hominy. One of my favorite ways of serving grits is in this spoon bread, which is very much like a soufflé or a baked Indian pudding. This wonderfully creamy custard-like spoon bread is a great alternative to mashed potatoes or steamed rice.

I cup cornmeal

I tablespoon baking powder

2 tablespoons cornstarch

1/2 teaspoon salt

1/2 teaspoon pepper

4 cups prepared hominy grits, cooled

2 tablespoons unsalted butter

5 large egg yolks, room temperature

I cup whole milk

1/2 teaspoon Tabasco sauce

5 large egg whites, room temperature

1/2 teaspoon cream of tartar

Oven temperature 375°F.

First, butter a 2-quart ceramic baking dish or casserole.

Second, combine the cornmeal with the baking powder, cornstarch, salt, and pepper in a small bowl. Whisk together thoroughly and set aside.

Third, use a wooden spoon to beat the butter into the cooked grits in a large mixing bowl. Next, stir in the egg yolks until they are fully incorporated, and then fold in the milk and Tabasco sauce. Finally, add the combined dry ingredients in 2 batches, mixing until smooth.

Fourth, use an electric handheld mixer to beat the egg whites with the cream of tartar in a separate bowl until they hold stiff peaks—to achieve the best results, be sure that your egg whites are at room temperature and the clean bowl is thoroughly dry. Gently fold the egg whites into the cornmeal mixture using a rubber spatula; stir until just combined.

Fifth, pour the batter into the prepared pan and bake until puffed and golden, about 45 minutes. Serve immediately.

MOLASSES-PECAN CAKE *with* CARAMEL BUTTERCREAM FROSTING

12 Servings

Pecan trees still grow wild throughout the southern United States, where they were planted by various Native American tribes from Mississippi to the Texas Hill Country. There are so many different, scrumptious pecan desserts to be found it is difficult to choose just one. Butter-rich, densely textured and with a gooey-nutty caramel flavor, this is some kind of cake—a cake lavished with all the German influence the Hill Country offers. It would make Oma proud!

Note: This cake is best when it is made the day before. Cover the cake with a dome or bowl and keep at room temperature for up to one day before serving.

CAKE

3 cups cake flour

1 tablespoon baking powder

1/2 teaspoon salt

1 cup (2 sticks) unsalted butter, softened

1 cup granulated sugar

1 cup packed dark brown sugar

1 1/2 teaspoons pure vanilla extract

4 large eggs, room temperature

2/3 cup strong-brewed coffee

1/3 cup molasses

1 cup finely ground pecans

CARAMEL BUTTERCREAM FROSTING

2 cups (4 sticks) unsalted butter, room temperature

1/4 cup granulated sugar

3 large egg whites, room temperature

1/8 teaspoon cream of tartar

1 1/2 cups dark brown sugar

2 teaspoons pure vanilla extract

1/2 cup water

1 (14-ounce) can sweetened condensed milk

1 cup chopped pecans

Oven temperature 350°F.

Make the cake: First, butter and flour two 9-inch round cake pans with 2-inch sides, tapping out the excess flour. Sift the cake flour, baking powder, and salt into a small bowl and set aside.

Second, thoroughly cream the butter with the granulated sugar and brown sugar until light and fluffy, 6 to 8 minutes. Beat in the vanilla. Reduce the speed to medium, and add the eggs one at a time, mixing well after each addition. Scrape down the sides of the bowl with a rubber spatula.

Third, combine the black coffee with the molasses. With the mixer running at low speed, alternately add the flour mixture and the coffee mixture in batches, beginning and ending with the flour, until fully combined. Fold in the ground pecans.

Fourth, divide the batter evenly between the two pans. Place the pans on the middle oven rack and bake until the cakes are beginning to shrink from the edges of the pans and the centers spring back when pressed gently, 20 to 25 minutes. Cool for 10 minutes. Loosen the cakes from their pans by running a thin knife around the edges, and then turn out onto the racks to cool completely.

Make the frosting: First, beat the butter until light and fluffy and set aside. Combine the granulated sugar, unbeaten egg whites, and cream of tartar in the bowl of a stand mixer. Set the mixing bowl over a pan of simmering water. Whisk by hand until the sugar is dissolved and the whites are warm, thick, and frothy, about 2 minutes. Transfer the bowl to the mixer and beat on medium-high speed until soft peaks form, about 3 minutes.

Second, combine the brown sugar, vanilla extract, and the water in a heavy-bottomed saucepan. Stir with a wooden spoon or heat-resistant spatula over medium-high heat until the sugar dissolves. Blend in the sweetened condensed milk. Continue cooking over medium-high heat, stirring constantly, until the caramel liquid reaches 234°F (soft ball stage), 4 to 5 minutes.

Third, turn the mixer to medium and begin to re-whip the egg whites. Carefully pour the hot caramel into the beaten egg white mixture in a slow, steady stream. Avoid pouring the caramel onto the beaters. Beat at medium-high speed until the frosting begins to cool, 15 to 20 minutes.

Fourth, add in the beaten butter, 1/4 cup at a time, beating well after each addition. If the first additions of butter begin to melt, cool a little longer, then continue mixing until the butter cream is smooth. Transfer the butter cream to a glass or stainless metal bowl, cover the surface with plastic wrap or buttered parchment paper until completely cooled to room temperature.

Assemble the cake: Mix together 1/3 of the buttercream with the chopped pecans. Place 1 layer of the cake on a serving platter or cake stand. Use an icing spatula or table knife to spread the filling evenly on the cake. Place the second layer over the first and cover the top and sides of the cake with the remaining frosting.

Easy Time-Saving and Do-Ahead Tips

SATURDAY:

- Cook the hominy grits and refrigerate them.

- Bake the cake layers. Prepare the buttercream and frost the cake.

- Pound the meat for the chicken fried steaks; seal in plastic wrap and refrigerate.

- Sift the dry ingredients for the spoon bread and the biscuits.

- Blanch the green beans and refrigerate.

SUNDAY MORNING:

- Prepare the spoon bread mixture for baking.

- Mix and bake the biscuits.

Chapter 10

NORTH COUNTRY FARE

SWEDISH-STYLE MEATBALLS
with SOUR CREAM GRAVY

HERB-SCENTED MUSHROOM WILD RICE

CAULIFLOWER *with* LEEKS *and* BACON

SWEET-AND-SOUR RED CABBAGE

SOUR CREAM-APPLE BUNDT CAKE

Along our northern border, among the great north woods, immigrants long ago began to build a new homeland. Although Vikings visited present-day Minnesota in 1362, the French were among the first to stay. They were followed by a wave of other groups—Germans and Scandinavians mostly—who further enriched the area with their traditions, social customs, and cooking styles.

These newcomers settled near the headwaters of the mighty Mississippi, along the St. Croix and St. Louis rivers, with easy outlets to the Great Lakes and the Mississippi waterway. St. Paul and her twin city, Minneapolis, soon became centers for manufacturing, mining, timber, and trade. The vast northern lands across the rugged Dakotas to Minnesota and Wisconsin were incorporated into our nation as part of the Louisiana Purchase.

I've traveled to the North Country many times. In the long summer nights, when evening spills into midnight, going out and enjoying good times with friends at the local eateries is the order of the day. But during the long cold winter months, gathering with family and friends around the warm glow of the fire and the warmth of a home-cooked meal comes to life.

Among the noted native harvests is wild rice, the seeds of the long marsh grass native to the western Great Lakes region. Native tribes harvested this grain and relied on it for sustenance and as a trading commodity. Life revolved around the wild rice harvest. Local tribes set up summer camps in the north to hunt game and gather the grains, wild berries, and mushrooms growing in the marshes and on the forest floors, which were dried and stored for winter meals. Several tribes created wild rice "farms" by wrapping the plants with ropes and sectioning off boundaries. Many tribal wars were fought over control of the marshes, but eventually the Chippewa became the dominant force. And though much of the wild rice is now produced in cultivated paddies, state laws still protect the Chippewa's access to the grain.

This cold climate and the native harvest seemed anything but unsuitable to the Norwegian and Swedish immigrants looking for a new home—perhaps they'd heard of this land passed down through ancient Viking lore. Like all travelers, foods and traditions from the homeland were carried to the new. Swedish meatballs, red cabbage, cold climate vegetables like cauliflower, and dense, moist cakes are among the dishes brought to this new northern land—now blended together with harvested native ingredients to create a new North Country fare.

SWEDISH-STYLE MEATBALLS
with SOUR CREAM GRAVY

6 Servings

This recipe is quite traditional—the centerpiece of a menu suitable anytime, but especially for an Advent or Twelfth Night celebration. Any variety of meats can be used. The north woods provide an abundance of wild game—venison, elk, moose, and duck—any of which can be substituted for the beef. And lean ground turkey breast is a great substitution for the veal.

MEATBALLS

1/2 pound lean ground beef

1/2 pound lean ground pork

1/2 pound lean ground veal

4 slices white bread, trimmed and cubed

1/2 cup cold milk

2 large eggs

2 tablespoons Dijon mustard

1 1/2 teaspoons salt

1 teaspoon ground pepper

Pinch ground nutmeg

1/2 cup dried breadcrumbs

1 medium onion, diced

2 tablespoons fresh chopped parsley

3 tablespoons butter

2 cups beef broth

2 teaspoons chopped capers, for garnish

GRAVY

3 tablespoons flour

1/4 cup water

Salt and pepper to taste

1/2 cup sour cream

Make the meatballs: First, in a large noncorrosive bowl, thoroughly mix the ground meats together.

Second, in a small bowl soak the bread cubes in the milk. In another small bowl whisk together the eggs, mustard, salt, pepper, and nutmeg.

Third, mix the egg mixture into the meat until well combined; then mix in the soaked bread, followed by the breadcrumbs, onion, and the parsley. Cover and refrigerate for at least one hour (this can be made a day in advance). Evenly divide and shape the mixture into 12 large meatballs.

Fourth, heat the butter in a large skillet over medium heat until it is melted and just beginning to bubble. Add in the meatballs, one by one, and cook for 6 to 8 minutes, turning occasionally, until they are evenly browned.

Finally, pour the beef broth into the skillet, cover with a tight-fitting lid, and reduce the heat to low. Simmer for 15 to 20 minutes, until the meatballs are done; transfer them to a clean platter.

Make the gravy: First, blend the flour with the water in a small bowl to form a smooth paste. Turn the burner to medium-high heat. Scrape the bottom and sides of the skillet with a stiff wire whisk to loosen any brown bits. When the liquid in the skillet begins to simmer, add about half of the flour paste, whisking constantly; add the remaining paste, a little at a time, until the gravy has thickened. Let the gravy simmer for 5 minutes. Then season to taste with salt and pepper. Whisk in the sour cream. Place the cooked meatballs in the gravy, and cover the skillet to keep them warm until you are ready to serve.

Garnish, if desired, with fresh chopped parsley or capers.

HERB-SCENTED MUSHROOM WILD RICE

6 Servings

Wild rice, which is known for its distinctly nutty flavor, is a perfect accompaniment to duck. The birds love to feed on this wild grain, so what could be more natural than serving them together? This is a really ethereal dish, with the heady mushrooms, leeks, and fresh herbs. It is also great paired with pheasant or quail, and especially good alongside game hen.

1 1/4 cups wild rice, thoroughly rinsed

4 cups lightly salted water

1/2 ounce dried wild mushrooms, soaked in warm water for 45 minutes

1/2 pound assorted fresh mushrooms, cleaned, tough, woody stems removed

1/4 cup duck fat or butter

1/2 cup diced celery

2 cloves garlic, chopped

1/2 cup chopped leeks (white part only)

1/2 cup diced onion

Pinch of salt

2 teaspoons fresh chopped rosemary

2 teaspoons fresh chopped thyme

1 cup chicken broth

Salt and pepper to taste

First, combine the rice and water in a heavy saucepan. Bring to a boil and reduce the heat to low; then cover with a tight-fitting lid and simmer, stirring occasionally, until the rice is tender but still firm and the grain has not yet split open, about 40 minutes. Drain, cool, and reserve.

Second, rinse and drain the wild mushrooms. Rough chop all of the mushrooms and combine.

Third, heat the duck fat in a skillet over medium heat and sauté the celery, garlic, leeks, and onion until the onion begins to brown, 4 to 5 minutes. Add in the chopped mushrooms, season with a pinch of salt, and toss with the rosemary and thyme; turn the heat to medium-low, cover the pan, and simmer until the mushrooms are tender, 2 to 3 minutes.

Fourth, toss in the parboiled wild rice and stir in the chicken broth. Raise the heat to medium, cover and simmer until the rice is fully cooked, 10 to 15 minutes. Season to taste with salt and pepper.

CAULIFLOWER *with* LEEKS *and* BACON

6 Servings

Cauliflower gets its snowy hue from the large leaves that shelter the head from sunlight. Select a head of cauliflower that is creamy–white and without spots or blemishes; make sure that the florets are firm and the leaves are green and still covering much of the flower.

1 small head cauliflower

2 medium leeks, white ends only

2 slices thick-cut bacon, cut into lardons

1 tablespoon butter

1/4 cup heavy cream

Salt and white pepper to taste

First, wash the head of cauliflower well. Remove the outer leaves and any small bruised sections. Use a paring knife to remove the core and break the cauliflower into florets.

Second, pour 1 inch of water into a saucepan and add the cauliflower florets. Cover the pan, bring the water to a boil, and steam until tender yet still firm, 5 to 6 minutes. Remove the pan from the heat, drain, and cool under cold running water.

Meanwhile, rinse the leeks thoroughly under cold running water to remove any grit; thinly slice the leeks and rinse well again.

Third, heat a skillet over medium heat, add in the bacon lardons and sauté for 2 to 3 minutes, just until the bacon is cooked but not brown. Melt the butter into the bacon drippings and add in the sliced leeks. Sauté the leeks until they are tender and translucent in color, 2 to 3 minutes.

Finally, increase the heat to medium-high, transfer the cauliflower to the skillet. Toss together with the leeks and bacon and pour in the cream. Season with salt and white pepper, and simmer for 3 to 4 minutes. Serve immediately.

SWEET-AND-SOUR RED CABBAGE

6 Servings ■■■■■■■■■■■■■■■■■■■■■■■■■■■■■■■■■

You'll love this sweet-and-sour red cabbage. It is especially great with dishes like sauerbraten. At our home we also serve it for Christmas alongside roast duck or venison. This can be made two or three days in advance and reheated in the microwave or on the stovetop.

1 small head of red cabbage

¹/2 cup red wine vinegar

2 tablespoons granulated sugar

2 teaspoons salt

2 tablespoons duck or bacon fat

1 medium apple, peeled, cored, and sliced

1 small onion, thinly sliced

1 bay leaf

1 whole clove

¹/4 cup red currant jelly

¹/2 cup boiling water

¹/4 cup dried cherries or cranberries

Salt and pepper to taste

First, rinse the head of cabbage under cold running water and remove the tough outer leaves. Slice into quarters and cut out the core. Thinly shred the cabbage using a serrated knife or food processor fitted with a steel blade. You should have 8 cups of shredded cabbage.

Second, place the shredded cabbage in a stainless mixing bowl. Sprinkle with the vinegar, sugar, and salt, and toss together until the cabbage is thoroughly coated.

Third, melt the duck or bacon fat over medium heat in a heavy 4-quart casserole or stainless pot. Add in the apple and onion slices, and sauté for 4 to 5 minutes, stirring frequently, until the onions are lightly browned. Add in the seasoned cabbage, bay leaf, and clove. Toss thoroughly and sauté for another 5 minutes. Lightly whisk together the red currant jelly and the boiling water in a small bowl, and then pour into the sweet-and-sour cabbage.

Fourth, cover the pot with a tight-fitting lid and reduce the heat to low. Check every so often to make sure the cabbage has enough moisture to keep it from sticking to the bottom of the pot. Add in a little more hot water, if needed. Simmer until the cabbage is tender but still has some bite left to it, 40 to 50 minutes. Ten to 15 minutes before the cabbage is finished cooking, add in the dried cherries or cranberries. The cabbage is done when it has turned a deep vibrant red, like the color of pickled beets, and all the liquid has been fully absorbed.

Finally, remove the bay leaf and clove. Adjust the seasoning to taste with salt and pepper, and transfer to your favorite serving bowl.

SOUR CREAM-APPLE BUNDT CAKE

12 Servings

The Bundt cake was invented in Minnesota, which might explain why one finds so many Bundt recipes in the Upper Midwest. With just the right hint of spice and crumbly goodness, this one is sure to become a family favorite. The cooked apples keep this rich, buttery cake really moist. I prefer to use mellow Golden Delicious apples, which stay firm and retain their shape when baked.

APPLES
6 medium Golden Delicious apples

1/4 cup (1/2 stick) unsalted butter

1/4 cup granulated sugar

1 teaspoon cardamom

BATTER
1/2 cup (1 stick) unsalted butter

2 cups all-purpose flour

1 1/4 cup granulated sugar

1/4 teaspoon allspice

2 teaspoons baking powder

1 teaspoon baking soda

1/2 teaspoon cinnamon

1/2 teaspoon salt

1 cup sour cream

2 large eggs, room temperature

1 teaspoon pure vanilla extract

Reserved syrup from the apples

1/2 cup fresh breadcrumbs

FOR THE PAN
2 tablespoons unsalted butter

1/2 cup fresh bread crumbs

Oven temperature 350°F.

Prepare the apples: Peel, core, and quarter the apples. Slice each quarter into 3 slices lengthwise. Melt the butter in a skillet over medium-low heat; when it begins to bubble, add in the apples, along with the sugar and cardamom, and sauté over low heat until the apples are tender but still firm, 3 to 4 minutes. Remove the apples from the heat, and cool to room temperature. Drain the apple slices and reserve the syrup—you should have 2 or 3 tablespoons.

Make the cake: First, melt the butter and cool to room temperature.

Second, in a large bowl combine the flour, sugar, allspice, baking powder, baking soda, cinnamon, and salt. Whisk together thoroughly.

Third, combine the cooled butter and sour cream in a separate bowl and beat until smooth. Add in the eggs and beat until they are fully blended.

Fourth, add the dry ingredients to the sour cream mixture, 1/2 cup at a time, mixing on low speed just long enough after each addition to fully incorporate. Scrape down the sides of the bowl with a spatula. Add in the vanilla and the reserved apple syrup; then increase the mixer speed to medium and beat for about 1 minute. Toss the cooked apple slices with the breadcrumbs and fold them into the batter.

Fifth, liberally butter a 9-inch Bundt pan with the 2 tablespoons butter and sprinkle the inside with the fresh breadcrumbs. Make sure the pan is completely coated before tapping out the excess.

Sixth, spoon the prepared batter into the Bundt pan. Place the pan on the middle oven rack, and bake for 50 to 60 minutes. When it is done, the cake should be pulling away from the edges of the pan and a wooden pick should come out clean when inserted. Cool on a wire rack for 20 minutes, and then run a thin metal spatula around the edges of the pan to loosen. Gently invert the cake onto the cooling rack and cool to room temperature.

To serve: If desired, lightly dust each slice with powdered sugar and serve with mounds of freshly whipped cream.

Easy Time-Saving and Do-Ahead Tips

SATURDAY :

- Parboil the wild rice and refrigerate covered in a stainless bowl.

- Bake the apple cake.

- Shred the red cabbage and cut the cauliflower and leeks; refrigerate in well-sealed containers.

SUNDAY MORNING:

- Prepare the meatball mixture.

Chapter 11

RETURN *to* THE HEARTLAND

CORNBREAD SAGE DRESSING

HERB-ROASTED CHICKEN *with*
NATURAL PAN JUICES

CREAMED PEAS *and* PEARL ONIONS

ROASTED CARROT *and* PARSNIP PURÉE

KNOTTED HONEY-WHOLE WHEAT ROLLS

HEARTLAND RAISIN-BUTTERMILK PIE

There's a reason we call the Midwest the heartland, and it's not just because it's in the center of the continent—in a sense, the sweeping region known as the Great Plains, with its heritage of hard work, self-reliance, and persevering faith, lives at the heart of American faith and values.

This vast area stretches from Indiana, Illinois, and Wisconsin across Iowa, Nebraska, and Kansas to eastern Colorado and the Dakotas. The landscape is mostly pancake flat or gently rolling, a subtle patchwork of farmland, pasture, and prairie under an enormous sky. This is the country of Frank Lloyd Wright, Laura Ingalls Wilder, and William Jennings Bryan; of quilting bees and county fairs; and of Holsteins and harvest moons. The land is written into our memories and celebrated in song for its tall grass, sweeping vistas, and amber waves of grain.

Early settlers were French—city names like Des Moines, Terra Haute, and St. Louis easily come to mind—when the prairies were part of the vast Louisiana territories. Much of America's heartland was settled during the great migration of the 1860s, when homesteading families arrived in droves to seek a better life. They were ambitious, self-reliant, do-it-yourself pioneers determined to carve a new homeland from the prairie. Soon they would be molded by the very land they sought to mold.

These were farmers who were used to working hard and performing the most difficult chores by themselves. Many came from Europe, especially Germany and the Scandinavian countries, fleeing poverty and war. Others ventured from homes back east in search of land and opportunity. They were Baptists, Amish, Mennonites, Lutherans, Methodists, and Quakers who saw their life of hard work as an expression of their quiet faith: A job worth doing was worth doing well.

Living here has always called for an extra portion of steadfast hope. These realities took firm hold in the hearts of those who lived in this area during the Great Depression, when drought baked the prairie, and the over-tilled soil blew away in great clouds. Those who stuck it out during the dust bowl developed particular habits of perseverance and thrift that shaped their very character.

Today we once again celebrate the heartland with satisfying and time-honored recipes that make good use of its bounty and resources. Wholesome, filling foods made with whole grains and corn, garden vegetables thriftily prepared, simple but delicious desserts—these are the pride of the Great Plains Sunday dinner table.

CORNBREAD SAGE DRESSING

8 Servings ■ ▪ ▪ ■ ▪ ■ ▪ ■ ▪ ▪ ■ ▪ ▪ ▪ ■ ▪ ■ ■ ▪ ■ ▪

Is it dressing or is it stuffing? That depends on which part of the country your family is from. In the South and Midwest, stuffing is dressing. In the Northeast dressing is stuffing. In my family, with its Southern roots—whether stuffed inside a bird or prepared on the stovetop— dressing was dressing and always made with cornbread.

¹/₂ cup (1 stick) unsalted butter

1 cup diced celery

1 cup diced onion

2 cups day-old bread cubes

1 tablespoon fresh chopped sage

4 cups packaged cornbread stuffing mix

¹/₄ teaspoon salt

¹/₄ teaspoon white pepper

1 teaspoon dry rubbed sage

2 ¹/₂ cups chicken broth

Oven temperature 350°F.

First, melt half the butter in a skillet over medium heat. Add the diced celery and onion, and sauté until the onions are soft and translucent, about 3 minutes. Make a well in the center of the pan by pushing the vegetables to the edges. Add in the remaining butter; when it begins to bubble, toss in the bread cubes, sprinkle the fresh sage over them and toss lightly for 1 minute, then stir together with the vegetables.

Third, combine the dry stuffing mix in a bowl with the salt, white pepper, and dried sage. Add in the sautéed bread cube mixture and toss together. Slowly add in the giblet stock, ¹/₄ cup at a time, tossing together after each addition to moisten the mix evenly. Place the cornbread mixture into a buttered over-proof ceramic casserole, cover, and bake for 35 minutes. For a crunchy, golden top, remove the cover after 20 minutes, brush with one or two tablespoons of butter, and continue baking for the final 15 minutes uncovered.

HERB-ROASTED CHICKEN
with NATURAL PAN JUICES

8 Servings ▪ ▬ ▪ ▬ ▪ ▬ ▪ ▬ ▪ ▬ ▪ ▬ ▪ ▬ ▪ ▬ ▪ ▬ ▪

This is roasted chicken at its very best! Simple and unadorned with the subtle use of sage and thyme,
and just a touch of grain mustard to bring out and accent the full flavor of the roasted chicken.

CHICKEN

2 whole chickens, 3 1/2 pounds each

2 tablespoons coarse salt, divided

2 ribs celery, chopped

4 cloves garlic, crushed

1 medium onion, chopped

1/2 bunch fresh sage

1/2 bunch fresh thyme

2 tablespoons extra virgin olive oil

2 tablespoons whole grain mustard

1 tablespoon chopped fresh sage

1 tablespoon chopped fresh thyme

NATURAL PAN JUICES

2 cups chicken broth

Salt and white pepper to taste

Oven temperature 350°F.

Prepare the chicken: First, rub the inside of each chicken with all but 2 teaspoons of the salt. Stuff each chicken cavity with the celery, garlic, onion, and bunches of fresh sage and thyme. Tuck the wings securely beneath the back of each chicken and tie the legs together with kitchen twine.

Second, combine the olive oil with the mustard in a small mixing bowl. Coat the outside of each chicken evenly with the mustard mixture, and sprinkle with the chopped herbs. Place the seasoned chickens in a shallow roasting pan, and season the outside with the remaining salt.

Third, place the roasting pan in the oven and roast for 1 1/2 to 1 3/4 hours. The chicken is done when a thermometer reads 165°F when inserted into the thickest part of the thigh. The drumstick should move up and down easily in its socket, and the juices should flow clear when a knife is inserted into the area between the leg and the thigh. Transfer the chicken to a clean cutting board, and allow it to rest at room temperature for 15 minutes before carving.

Prepare the pan juices: First, while the chicken is resting on the cutting board, pour the juices from the roasting pan into a cup and skim off the excess fat. Place the roasting pan over medium heat. Use a stiff wire whisk to scrape the drippings free and then add the pan juices back into the pan.

Second, blend in the 2 cups of chicken stock, reduce the heat to low, and simmer for 5 minutes. Season with salt and white pepper to taste.

Carve the chicken: Use a pair of kitchen shears to cut away the kitchen twines from the legs. Cut the chicken in half through the backbone and then through the breast bone. Use a kitchen spoon to remove and discard the vegetables and herbs from the cavity. Pull each leg up and away from the breast and slice the skin between the leg and the breast—the legs will come away easily—then cut between the drumstick and the thigh. Separate the wings from the breasts.

CREAMED PEAS *and* PEARL ONIONS

8 Servings

Tender peas and pearl onions, sweetened with just a touch of fresh cream and butter, are hard to beat for sheer simplicity. The addition of fresh mint and snipped chives results in near culinary perfection.

16 ounces (1 dry pint) pearl onions

2 tablespoons butter

4 cups fresh blanched peas or frozen peas, thawed

1/2 cup heavy cream

Salt to taste

1 tablespoon fresh snipped chives

1 teaspoon fresh chopped mint

First, place the onions in a medium bowl and cover them with boiling water. Steep for 5 minutes, then drain well; trim off the root ends with a paring knife and peel away the skin, leaving the onions whole.

Second, melt the butter in a small skillet over medium heat. When the butter just begins to bubble, add in the pearl onions and sauté for 2 minutes. Add in the peas and sauté for 1 minute more. Pour in the cream, season with salt, and simmer until the cream is reduced and beginning to thicken, 4 to 5 minutes.

Third, add in the chives and mint, and toss to combine. Serve immediately.

ROASTED CARROT *and* PARSNIP PURÉE

8 Servings

Roasting the carrots and parsnips brings out their natural sugars and adds a hint of caramel flavor, which is a perfect complement to their juicy sweetness.

2 pounds carrots, scrubbed

1 pound parsnips, scrubbed

12 tablespoons (1 1/2 sticks) butter, divided

Salt to taste

2 tablespoons packed brown sugar

1 cup apple juice or white grape juice

Oven temperature 350°F.

First, bake the carrots and parsnips on a lightly oiled baking sheet until they are just beginning to soften, about 1 hour. Cool them enough to handle and peel away the skins with a sharp paring knife or vegetable peeler. Cut into 1/2-inch-thick rounds.

Second, melt 4 tablespoons of the butter in a skillet over medium heat and sauté the roasted vegetables for 5 minutes. Season to taste with a little salt; add in the brown sugar and cook for another minute or so, stirring so that the sugar and butter combine thoroughly. Then pour in the apple or white grape juice and continue to cook over medium heat until the vegetables are completely cooked and the liquid has been reduced by half, 15 to 20 minutes. Turn off the heat and cover the pan until you are ready to purée.

Third, purée the vegetables in a food processor or grind through a food mill. Whip in the remaining 8 tablespoons of butter and adjust the salt to taste.

KNOTTED HONEY-WHOLE WHEAT ROLLS

18 Rolls

Robust whole-grain breads cooked on the open hearth are the hallmark of heartland baking. These breads have a simple, satisfying European influence that celebrates the bounty of the field.

1 package (1 1/2 teaspoons) active dry yeast

1/4 cup warm water, about 110°F

1 cup whole milk

1/4 cup (1/2 stick) unsalted butter

1/4 cup honey

1 large egg, room temperature, lightly beaten

2 cups whole wheat flour, divided

1 1/2 cups all-purpose flour

1/2 cup wheat germ

2 teaspoons salt

Oven temperature 400°F.

First, sprinkle the yeast over the warm water and let the mixture stand for 1 minute, then stir until the yeast is dissolved.

Second, heat the milk in a small saucepan to the point of boiling; remove it from the heat and swirl in the butter until it is melted. Cool in the pan until lukewarm.

Third, combine the yeast with the lukewarm milk. Blend in the honey and the lightly beaten egg. Using a wooden spoon, stir in 1 cup of the whole wheat flour and then 1 cup of the all-purpose flour. The mixture should be the consistency of thick batter. Continue stirring for about 200 strokes; scrape down the sides of the bowl with a rubber spatula. Cover with a clean tea towel and set in a draft-free place until it is bubbly and has doubled in volume, about 2 hours.

Fourth, in a separate mixing bowl combine the remaining 1 cup whole wheat flour and 1/2 cup all-purpose flour with the wheat germ and the salt. Blend thoroughly with a stiff wire whisk.

Fifth, transfer the bubbly mixture to the bowl of an electric mixer fitted with a dough hook. Turn the speed to low, and slowly add in the blended flour mixture, half a cup at a time; scrape down the sides of the bowl between additions. Increase the mixer speed to medium and add in a little extra flour as necessary, until the dough pulls away from the sides of the bowl and forms a ball. At this point the dough will be firm and densely textured. Reduce the mixer speed to low and knead for 10 minutes.

Sixth, divide the dough into 18 equal pieces. Roll each piece between the palms of your hands into a 5- to 6-inch rope. Tie each rope loosely into a simple knot and place on a lightly greased baking sheet. Cover the rolls with a clean tea towel that has been dusted with a little flour. Set the rolls in a draft-free place, and let them rise until they have doubled in size, about 1 to 1^1/$_2$ hours (or 2 hours, if they were refrigerated).

Finally, lightly brush the tops with a little milk and bake for 12 to 15 minutes. Brush the tops with a little butter before serving.

HEARTLAND RAISIN-BUTTERMILK PIE

8 Servings

The tangy buttermilk brings a bit of zest to this simple, unadorned Old World custard pie. The sweet, buttery pie crust is more in keeping with the tradition of central European pastries, and the addition of zesty lemon is an excellent surprise.

PIE CRUST

I cup all-purpose flour

1/4 cup granulated sugar

1/2 teaspoon salt

1/4 cup (1/2 stick) unsalted butter

I large egg yolk, room temperature

I teaspoon pure vanilla extract

I to 2 tablespoons cold water, as needed

BUTTERMILK FILLING

2/3 cup dark raisins

3 large eggs, room temperature

2 tablespoons unsalted butter, softened

I cup granulated sugar

2 cups buttermilk

1/4 cup all-purpose flour

I teaspoon pure vanilla extract

2 tablespoons fresh lemon juice

Zest of I lemon

1/4 teaspoon nutmeg

Oven temperature 400°F.

Make the crust: First, whisk the flour, sugar, and salt together using a stiff wire whisk. Cut in the butter with a pastry cutter, or pulse for several seconds in a food processor until the mixture reaches the consistency of coarse crumbly meal.

Then add in the egg yolk, vanilla, and a sparse tablespoon of cold water, and mix just long enough for the dough to hold together. Add a few extra drops of water as needed for the dough to reach the consistency of cookie dough. Roll into a ball, flatten into a disk, and wrap in plastic. Chill the dough in the refrigerator for at least 20 minutes and up to 5 days.

Second, sprinkle a clean dry surface with a little flour and roll the chilled dough into a 12-inch circle. Brush off any excess flour, then line a 9-inch pie or tart pan with the dough and chill in the refrigerator for 30 minutes.

Third, line the chilled crust with foil, fill it with pie weights or dried beans and bake for 10 minutes. Cool on a baking rack and remove the foil and pie weights. The crust will be partially baked and have a pale golden hue.

Reduce the oven temperature to 350°F.

Make the filling: First, plump the raisins by soaking them for 30 minutes in a bowl of warm water. Drain thoroughly and set aside.

Second, whisk together the eggs, butter, and sugar in a mixing bowl. Place the buttermilk in a small saucepan, and whisk in the flour until smooth. Heat the buttermilk mixture, stirring constantly, until it just begins to thicken and bubble. Stir 1/2 cup of the thickened buttermilk into the egg mixture to temper it, and then blend both together completely.

Third, whisk in the vanilla, lemon juice, and zest, and add in the plumped raisins. Pour the filling into the pre-baked pie shell, and sprinkle the nutmeg on top.

Fourth, bake the pie for 30 to 35 minutes. The pie is done when the custard has begun to rise evenly and a knife inserted into the custard comes out clean. The pie can be cooled to room temperature and served immediately, or it can be made the day before and chilled overnight, covered.

Easy Time-Saving and Do-Ahead Tips

SATURDAY:

- Blanch the peas (if using fresh) and peel the pearl onions; refrigerate in well-sealed containers.

- Roast the carrots and parsnips.

- Prepare the ingredients for the sage stuffing.

- Mix together the pie crust and refrigerate.

- Make the buttermilk filling for the pie and bake.

SUNDAY MORNING:

- Prepare the dough for the rolls; cover and refrigerate.

THREE HOURS BEFORE DINNER:

- Remove the rolls from the refrigerator to rise.

Chapter 12

A TIMELESS SENSIBILITY

BROAD BEANS *and* TOMATOES

OLD-FASHIONED YANKEE POT ROAST
with ROOT CELLAR VEGETABLES

PARKER HOUSE ROLLS

VICTORIAN GINGERBREAD

Call it merchant savvy or Yankee ingenuity—this energetic blend of enterprise, industry, and plain old common sense helped shape the American character and define the American experience. From the time the Dutch East India Company financed an expedition to America (ten years before the Pilgrims landed at Plymouth Rock) and purchased the lands that are now Manhattan Island, commerce has been the lifeblood of this land we call home.

Merchant savvy and Yankee know-how continued to flourish in the nineteenth century, but it was always balanced by a powerful love of home and family. The home was the center of Victorian-era city life, an oasis from the busy workaday world. While city life bustled outside, the interior of the house glowed with warmth. Homemaking was elevated to a fine craft and celebrated in publications like *Godey's Lady's Book* and *The American Woman's Home*. Crafts, music, family games, and story time were the hallmarks of a serene, well-ordered life. And Sunday was always special—a day of lingering charm, white linen and lace, content and secure children, providence and protection. Families enjoyed a wholesome afternoon filled with fun and frolic, relished long into the evening and hushed only by the fall of night.

The Victorian era was known for its public gardens and parks—this was an era of social responsibility, moderation, and discovery. An emerging middle class, grounded in a desire for a better quality of life and more healthful living, brought into fashion community and home boxed-gardens. Less meat and meals ample with locally grown and seasonal produce became the standard. Home-canning and new modern kitchen gadgets brought to the homemaker's tasks more craft and pleasure.

Our world today is not so different. We busily engage in commerce and pursue excellence in our chosen vocations. We work hard, and our children study hard—but to what end, if we don't take pleasure in just a few uninterrupted hours together one day a week?

Today, those of us living amid the urban renewal celebrate these shared timeless sensibilities. The slow-food movement and farm-to-table initiatives remind us that "all things in moderation" are good. A hearty, juicy pot roast surrounded by root cellar vegetables and a warm-from-the-oven slice of gingerbread crowned with a mound of sweetened whipped cream offer something more than just good food—they remind us that simple pleasures shared with family and friends are worthy pursuits. What could possibly be more important?

BROAD BEANS *and* TOMATOES

8 Servings ■ ▪ ■ ▪ ▪ ■ ▪ ■ ▪ ■ ▪ ■ ▪ ■ ▪ ■ ▪ ■ ▪ ■ ▪ ■

Tomatoes were introduced into New England cooking in the late eighteenth century. In 1887 the U.S. Supreme Court, in a trade dispute, ruled that tomatoes are a vegetable. Indeed, paired with broad beans—both of which remain staples of the home garden—they are a perfect accompaniment to pot roast.

6 medium ripe tomatoes

1 pound broad beans

1 tablespoon butter

1 medium onion, thinly sliced

1/2 teaspoon granulated sugar

Salt and ground black pepper

1 tablespoon fresh chopped flat-leaf parsley

First, bring a large pot of water to a rolling boil. Using a sharp knife carefully cut an X across the skin on the smooth bottom end of the tomato. Drop the tomatoes 2 or 3 at a time into the boiling water, just until the skin begins break away from the flesh, about 30 seconds. Immediately, plunge them into a bowl of ice water. Carefully peel the skin away with a paring knife. Cut the tomatoes in half. Remove the stem and the seeds.

Second, trim the ends of the beans and pull any tough strings. Using the same pot of boiling water, blanch the beans just long enough to turn bright green, 3 to 4 minutes. Drain the beans and immediately plunge them into ice water.

Third, melt the butter in a skillet. Add in the slivered onion and sauté over low heat until translucent, 3 to 4 minutes. Cut the tomatoes into chunks and toss them together with the onion. Sprinkle the onions and tomatoes with the sugar, and sauté for 1 to 2 minutes more. Add in the blanched beans, and season with salt and pepper. Increase the heat to medium and sauté until the beans are cooked through and the onions and tomatoes have begun to caramelize, 4 to 5 minutes. Toss with the parsley.

OLD-FASHIONED YANKEE POT ROAST *with* ROOT CELLAR VEGETABLES

8 Servings

Chuck roast is the best cut for making pot roast; its marbled fat tenderizes the meat during cooking and keeps it moist. A bottom-round roast works well too, but today's lean beef tends to become dry when cooked beyond medium. Like most braised meats, pot roast is best when cooked in a Dutch oven or a heavy cast-iron pan finished in enamel.

POT ROAST

1 (4- to 5-pound) beef chuck roast, 2 inches thick

2 teaspoons salt

1 teaspoon coarse-ground black pepper

Vegetable oil

2 cups beef broth

1 cup water, as needed

1 bay leaf

2 cloves garlic, sliced

1 teaspoon fresh chopped marjoram leaves

VEGETABLES

4 large carrots

4 ribs celery

2 large onions

2 large turnips

8 medium potatoes

Salt and pepper to taste

GRAVY

3 tablespoons all-purpose flour

1/2 cup water

Salt and pepper to taste

Oven temperature 300°F.

Prepare the roast: First, season the meat with the salt and pepper. Allow the seasoned meat to come to room temperature, about 20 minutes.

Second, add just enough oil to lightly coat the bottom of a Dutch oven or braising pan fitted with a lid, and heat over medium-high heat. When the oil is just beginning to smoke, reduce the temperature to medium; add the meat and brown it slowly, turning it every minute or so. When the roast is evenly browned on all sides, pour in all the beef broth and just enough water to cover the roast a little more than halfway; add in the bay leaf, sliced garlic, and marjoram.

Third, cover the pan and heat the liquid to a simmer. Transfer to the bottom rack of your oven.

Prepare the vegetables: First, peel the carrots and cut into 1¹/2-inch-thick rounds. Trim the celery and cut into 1-inch pieces. Peel the onions and cut into quarters. Peel the turnips and cut into quarters. Peel the potatoes and cut in half.

Second, after the roast has been cooking for 2 hours, test the meat to be sure it is tender by gently inserting a fork into the thickest part. If the roast does not yield easily to the fork, add a little water as needed and continue cooking until the fork can be inserted effortlessly. Then add all the vegetables except for the potatoes into the liquid around the roast; replace the lid, bring to a simmer, and cook on top of the stove for another 15 minutes.

Third, place the potatoes on top of the vegetables, season with a little salt and pepper, replace the lid and return to the oven for the final 45 minutes or until the potatoes are done. At this point the meat should be tender, just falling away from the fat and easy to pull apart from each section, but still firm enough to slice.

Fourth, let the roast rest in the pan at room temperature for 10 minutes, and then transfer the roast and vegetables to a platter. Cover with foil to keep warm and leave the cooking liquid in the roasting pan.

Prepare the gravy: First, combine the flour with the water in a small bowl and use a stiff wire whisk to form a smooth paste.

Second, place the roasting pan with the cooking liquid over medium-high heat. When the liquid begins to simmer, add in about half of the paste, whisking constantly. Add more paste, a little at a time, until the gravy thickens to the desired consistency. Turn the heat to low, let the gravy simmer for 5 minutes, and season to taste with salt and pepper.

To serve: Transfer the roast to a clean cutting board and use a sharp knife to slice the roast across the grain. Serve the pot roast on the platter, garnished with the vegetables. Pass the gravy separately in a gravy boat.

PARKER HOUSE ROLLS

18 Rolls ▪ ■ ▪ ■ ▪ ■ ▪ ■ ▪ ■ ▪ ■ ▪ ■ ▪ ■ ▪ ■ ▪ ■ ▪ ■

The Parker House in Boston was founded by coachman Harvey Parker and has been in operation since opening its doors in 1855. On one memorable occasion, Charles Dickens, Henry Longfellow, Oliver Wendell Holmes, and Ralph Waldo Emerson dined together there. Perhaps they enjoyed these rolls, which are now an American classic.

1 package (1 1/2 teaspoons) active dry yeast

1/4 cup warm water, about 110°F

1 cup whole milk

2 tablespoons granulated sugar

7 tablespoons unsalted butter, divided

3 cups all-purpose flour, divided

1 teaspoon salt

Oven temperature 400°F.

First, sprinkle the yeast over the warm water and let the mixture stand for 1 minute; then stir until the yeast is dissolved.

Second, heat the milk with the sugar just to the point of boiling in a small saucepan, and then remove the pan from heat. Add 3 tablespoons of butter and swirl until the butter has melted. Cool the mixture in the saucepan until lukewarm.

Third, combine the yeast mixture with the lukewarm milk in a mixing bowl and stir in 2 cups of the flour. The mixture will now be the consistency of a thick batter. Continue stirring for about 120 strokes. Cover the bowl with a clean tea towel and set in a draft-free place until it is bubbly and has doubled in volume, about 1 hour.

Fourth, whisk the remaining flour into the salt using a stiff wire whisk. Use an electric mixer fitted with a dough hook to slowly incorporate the flour mixture into the bubbly dough on low speed. Scrape down the sides of the bowl with a rubber spatula. Increase the mixer speed to medium and add in a little extra flour as necessary, until the dough begins to pull away from the sides of the bowl and form a ball. Reduce the mixer speed to low, and knead the dough for about 5 minutes. The dough will have a smooth soft texture. Dust the dough with a little flour to keep it from sticking to your hands. Form it into a ball, place in a lightly oiled bowl, and cover with plastic wrap. Refrigerate for at least 30 minutes.

Fifth, melt the remaining 4 tablespoons of butter in a shallow bowl. Divide the dough into 18 equal pieces and roll them into balls. Place the balls on a clean dry surface that has been dusted with a little flour. Sprinkle the balls with a little more flour and flatten each with the palm of your hand. Brush each generously with the melted butter and fold in half.

Sixth, place the rolls about 2 inches apart on a lightly greased baking sheet. Let the rolls rise in a draft-free place until they have doubled in size, about 1 hour. Bake for 12 to 15 minutes. Brush with any remaining melted butter.

VICTORIAN GINGERBREAD

9 Servings ■▬▬■▬▬■▬■▬■▬■▬■▬■▬■▬■▬■▬■▬■▬

Gingerbread has been made in this country since **The Mayflower** *first arrived, and it reached the height of popularity during the Victorian years. Gingerbread was originally served alongside baked beans and roast pork, rather than as a dessert. My grandmother always substituted hot coffee for the water found in most recipes; she did the same with her delicious old-fashioned applesauce cake.*

I love eating gingerbread warm out of the oven, topped with freshly whipped cream.

2 ¹/4 cups all-purpose flour

2 teaspoons baking soda

I teaspoon ground cinnamon

¹/2 teaspoon ground cloves

2 teaspoons ground ginger

¹/2 teaspoon salt

²/3 cup shortening

²/3 cup packed light brown sugar

3/4 cup molasses

2 large eggs, room temperature, well beaten

I cup hot coffee

Oven temperature 375°F.

First, grease and lightly flour a 9 x9 x 2-inch baking pan.

Second, whisk the flour, baking soda, cinnamon, cloves, ginger, and salt together in a mixing bowl and set aside.

Third, combine the shortening and brown sugar in the bowl of an electric mixer fitted with a paddle. Beat together at medium speed for 3 to 4 minutes. Pour in the molasses, and scrape down the sides of the bowl with a rubber spatula. Slowly add in the beaten eggs and mix until they are fully incorporated into the batter, about 1 minute.

Fourth, turn the mixer speed down to low. Add in the dry ingredients, ¹/2 cup at a time, mixing after each addition for about 10 seconds. When ²/3 of the dry ingredients are mixed in, quickly pour in half of the hot coffee, followed by the remaining dry ingredients, and finally the remaining coffee. Mix until just combined.

Fifth, scrape down the sides of the bowl with a rubber spatula and beat by hand until smooth, 20 to 30 strokes. Pour the batter into the prepared baking pan. Place the pan on the middle oven rack. Bake until a cake tester or wooden pick comes out clean, though still a little moist, when inserted into the middle, 40 to 45 minutes. Cool the cake in the pan.

To serve: Cut the gingerbread into 9 equal pieces. Serve, if desired, with mounds of sweetened freshly whipped cream.

Easy Time-Saving and Do-Ahead Tips

SATURDAY:

- Bake the gingerbread.

- Prepare the vegetables for the pot roast and refrigerate in well-sealed containers.

SUNDAY MORNING:

- Prepare the dough for the rolls and refrigerate.

- Remove the pot roast from the refrigerator, season and bring to room temperature.

- Brown the pot roast and begin cooking in the oven.

ONE HOUR BEFORE DINNER:

- Bake the rolls.

- Prepare the tomatoes and beans.

Chapter 13

IN THE
NEIGHBORHOOD

BRAISED SWISS CHARD

BRAISED PAPRIKA VEAL SHANKS

HOMEMADE EGG NOODLES *with*
PARSLEY *and* TOMATO BUTTER

WARM PEAR STRUDEL *with* VANILLA SAUCE

America was once a country of neighborhoods. Even in the biggest cities, life typically revolved around neighborhood schools and churches, local bakeries, butcher shops, grocers, bookstores, restaurants, and so on. Each neighborhood had its own distinctive flavor. There were Catholic or Jewish or Muslim neighborhoods, and each was energized by rich traditions. The people were Irish or Czech or Chinese, white or black, united by a shared culture and shared problems. Yes, these neighborhoods could be insular or exclusive—they could inspire stereotypes—but they also offered people an oasis of familiarity in an overwhelming sea of change. Each, too, added its own rich flavoring to the melting pot that is America.

More and more these days, we see ourselves first as Americans. And we should. We are from so many places, of so many faiths, yet we are still united by the ideal of freedom. We are "one nation under God." Many of us claim such diversity in our heritage that *American* really is the only possible label. But that very diversity is still something to appreciate and preserve.

In many ways the homogenization of America is a sad reality. Colorless suburbs, featureless fast-food restaurants, indistinguishable chain-store shopping malls, and familiar logos diminish the unique character for which neighborhoods were once known. But surely the key to healing our divisions lies in allowing our differences to enrich us all, not washing out those differences in a sea of sameness.

The flavors that make up the traditional American table, the foods from our neighborhoods, celebrate our diversity and provide a window to our varied but united past. Indeed, our melting pot is a simmering, savory dish made from a wide variety of tasty ingredients.

So take a Sunday walk with me through an old neighborhood in all its particular glory. Picture, if you will, little markets with meats hanging in the window. Squeeze some fruit at the greengrocers, and admire the glossy array of vegetables: garlic, leeks, turnips, tomatillos. Stand on the corner and listen to the gossip as the intoxicating aromas from little restaurants and bakeries drift down the block, beckoning us with every passing breeze. Lift a lid in a kitchen to enjoy the old-world ambience of slow-braised veal with garlic and paprika, aromatic herbs and vegetables, or even mushrooms. And smile, because this is America in all her diverse glory; it's a Sunday celebration straight from the heart of the neighborhood.

BRAISED SWISS CHARD

6 Servings

Swiss chard are wonderful greens, with a sweet flavor and crunchy texture. They are especially good wilted and seasoned with a splash of vinegar. Sliced apples or a little orange juice can also be a great addition.

2 bunches Swiss chard

¼ cup (½ stick) butter

¼ cup thinly sliced red onion

I tablespoon tarragon or sherry vinegar

Salt and pepper to taste

First, wash the chard thoroughly in several changes of cool running water to remove any bits of dirt. Remove and discard any wilted or brown leaves and cut off any dry ends from the stalks. Cut each stalk into three or four leafy pieces.

Second, heat the butter in a large skillet over medium heat until it is melted and bubbling. Add in the sliced onion and sauté for 1 minute. Add the chard and pour in the vinegar. Cover the skillet and steam for 2 to 3 minutes, tossing the chard occasionally so that it wilts evenly. Season to taste with salt and pepper.

BRAISED PAPRIKA VEAL SHANKS

6 Servings ■

One of the best cuts for braising is the shank—particularly lamb or veal. The shank is the lean calf muscle of the leg. Shanks have long been underappreciated cuts of meat, but they are still enjoyed in neighborhoods where skilled butchers carefully trim and prepare select pieces from whole sides hung cold and aged to perfection.

Have your butcher cut the veal shanks into 1¹/₂-inch-thick slices and tie each piece securely with kitchen twine to retain its shape. Each slice should be about 4 inches in diameter and weigh about 12 ounces, a hearty portion.

VEAL SHANKS

6 pieces cut veal shank

Salt and white pepper

1 tablespoon olive oil

2 tablespoons butter

1 carrot, peeled and chopped

1 rib celery, chopped

4 whole cloves garlic

1 leek, white part only, chopped

1 small onion, quartered

2 tablespoons tomato paste

2 tablespoons all-purpose flour

1 cup dry white wine

2 cups veal or chicken broth

1 bay leaf

1 tablespoon paprika

2 sprigs fresh thyme

4 to 5 white peppercorns

Salt and pepper to taste

MUSHROOM SAUCE

2 tablespoons (¹/₄ stick) butter

8 ounces sliced button mushrooms

1 medium onion, thinly sliced

Pinch of salt

¹/₄ cup dry white wine

¹/₂ cup sour cream

Salt and pepper to taste

Oven temperature 300°F.

Prepare the veal shanks: First, season the veal with the salt and white pepper. Heat the oil in a Dutch oven or braising pan with a tight-fitting lid over medium-high heat. When the oil just begins to smoke, add the meat to the skillet and sear the shanks until they are evenly browned, 4 to 5 minutes per side. Transfer the shanks to a warm platter and tent with foil to keep them warm.

Second, add the butter to the casserole that was used for the veal; when it is melted, scatter in the carrot, celery, garlic, leek, and onion. Sauté the vegetables until they begin to brown, 4 to 5 minutes.

Third, whisk the tomato paste into the vegetables; then sprinkle in the flour and whisk to form a roux. Pour in the wine and allow the wine to cook for 1 to 2 minutes. When the mixture becomes thick and bubbly, add the broth, bay leaf, paprika, thyme, and peppercorns. Return the shanks to the pan, cover with a tight-fitting lid, and place the pan on the bottom rack of the oven. Braise for 1¹/₂ to 2 hours. The meat should be tender and just beginning to pull away from the bone, but still firm.

Fourth, transfer the shanks from the casserole to a warm platter. Skim off any excess fat that may have risen to the top of the sauce. Strain the remaining sauce through a fine sieve into a small bowl, pressing on the vegetables with a rubber spatula so that all the flavorful juices are extracted. Discard the vegetables and season the sauce to taste with salt and pepper. Reduce the oven to 200°F.

Prepare the mushroom sauce: Melt the butter over medium heat in the same casserole that was used for the veal. When the butter begins to bubble, add the mushrooms and sliced onion, and season with a pinch of salt. Sauté until the onion slices are translucent and the mushrooms are tender, 2 to 3 minutes. Pour in the wine and simmer for 1 to 2 more minutes. Blend in the sauce reserved from the veal; then carefully remove the kitchen twine from the shanks and add the veal to the sauce. Cover the pan and transfer the shanks to the oven for 20 minutes before serving.

Serve the shanks: Transfer the shanks to a warm serving platter. Whisk the sour cream into the sauce and season to taste. Lace the shanks with sauce, and serve the remainder of the sauce in a gravy boat.

HOMEMADE EGG NOODLES *with* PARSLEY *and* TOMATO BUTTER

6 Servings

Making noodles is a bit of work, but oh, what a difference! Like so much of home cooking, it is all about love. It can also be fun to make noodles with the kids; they will come to appreciate the time and care good cooking takes, especially because the rewards are in the eating. You can, of course, substitute fresh store-bought noodles when time is a factor.

EGG NOODLES

2 cups all-purpose flour

1/2 teaspoon salt

2 large eggs, lightly beaten

1/4 cup whole milk

TOMATO BUTTER

1/2 cup (1 stick) butter

2 cloves garlic, minced

1/4 cup minced onion

1 cup peeled, seeded, and diced fresh tomatoes

1 tablespoon fresh chopped parsley

1/2 cup dry white wine

Salt and pepper to taste

Make the noodles: First, sift the flour together with the salt into a large shallow mixing bowl. Beat the eggs with the milk in a separate bowl. Make a well in the center of the flour and slowly pour the liquid ingredients into the well. Use a dinner fork to gently blend the flour into the beaten eggs by whisking the eggs in a circular motion and drawing the flour into the eggs, a tablespoon at a time (the process should take 10 to 12 minutes). The mixture will at first become a thick liquid, then a soft dough, and finally reach the firmness of pastry dough.

Once the soft dough begins to form, use the tips of your fingers to roll the dough in a circular motion until there is just a thin rim of flour left around the edges of the bowl. Form the dough into a ball, and knead in the remaining flour, as well as any bits of dough stuck to the bottom of the bowl. Knead until the dough is the consistency of pie pastry and just a little sticky to the fingers when pressed. If needed, add a little more flour.

Second, turn the ball of dough onto a clean work surface that has been lightly dusted with flour. Continue kneading, pressing the dough firmly with the heel of your hand to flatten the ball, folding it in half back over itself so it is doubled up again and pressing flat again in a continuous motion for 8 to 10 minutes, until completely smooth.

Third, allow the dough to rest for 20 minutes covered with a clean tea towel. Flatten and shape the dough in as close to a square as possible; divide the dough into 4 equal pieces. Press the pieces one at a time onto a clean work surface that has been lightly dusted with flour and flatten with a rolling pin. Lightly dust the dough with flour and roll out into 12 x 5-inch rectangles that are a little less than 1/16-inch thick (about half the thickness of pie dough). Use a knife or pizza wheel to cut the dough, guiding with a ruler or straightedge, into 1/2-inch-wide, 5-inch-long noodles. If the noodles aren't thin enough, don't worry—simply lay each noodle flat on the work surface and give it one firm roll to attain the desired thinness. The noodles won't have the same uniform cut, but this method will be well worth the extra effort.

Fourth, transfer the noodles to a pasta rack or lay them flat on sheets of waxed paper. Let the noodles dry for about 1 hour.

Cook the noodles: Drop them into a large pot of boiling salted water. After 1 minute, separate the noodles gently with a cooking fork so that they don't stick to the bottom of the pot or each other. Cook until tender yet firm (al dente), about 5 minutes. Drain thoroughly and set aside.

Make the tomato butter: Melt the butter in a skillet over medium heat until it just begins to bubble. Add the garlic and onion, and sauté until translucent, 2 to 3 minutes. Add the tomatoes and parsley, and sauté for about 1 minute. Pour in the wine and simmer for 2 to 3 minutes. Season to taste with salt and pepper.

Prepare the dish: Shake any excess water from the noodles and add them to the sauce. (If the noodles stick together in the colander, run a little hot water over them and shake off the excess water.) Toss together well and adjust the seasoning to taste. Transfer to a wide bowl and serve immediately.

WARM PEAR STRUDEL
with VANILLA SAUCE

6 Servings

There are few desserts in the world as satisfying as warm, freshly prepared strudel. Making the delicate dough by hand is something else altogether: You must slowly stretch it over a linen sheet and carefully pull it until it is thin and silky enough to read a newspaper through. It is something everyone should try at least once. After gaining an appreciation for all the work involved, you'll gratefully go back to using store-bought sheets of phyllo, as we do in this recipe.

VANILLA SAUCE

3 large egg yolks, room temperature

1 teaspoon pure vanilla extract

1/2 cup granulated sugar

1 cup half-and-half

1/2 cup heavy cream

FILLING

4 medium firm ripe pears

Lemon juice

1/4 cup dried currants

2 tablespoons all-purpose flour

2 tablespoons granulated sugar

1/4 teaspoon ground allspice

STRUDEL

1/2 cup (1 stick) unsalted butter

1 tablespoon vegetable oil

8 sheets frozen phyllo dough

3 tablespoons ground hazelnuts

6 tablespoons fresh white bread crumbs

1 tablespoon granulated sugar

Make the vanilla sauce: First, combine the egg yolks and vanilla in a stainless bowl or in the top of a double boiler. Slowly beat in the sugar with a wire whisk—it's important that the sugar is dissolved slowly and completely into the yolks (beating the mixture too rapidly will make the yolks frothy and full of air).

Second, scald the half-and-half and the cream in a small saucepan over medium heat just to the point of boiling and remove from the heat immediately. Temper the yolks by whisking 1/2 cup of the hot cream into the yolk mixture until fully blended. Then whisk in the remaining hot cream.

Third, place the bowl over a pan of simmering water, making sure that the bowl does not touch the water. Cook the sauce, stirring constantly with a heat-resistant rubber spatula, until thickened, 6 to 8 minutes. To test for thickness, dip a spoon into the sauce and hold it horizontally over the pan, making sure that the sauce coats the spoon evenly. Run your finger through the sauce on the spoon—if the line doesn't fill back up, it has thickened enough. Strain through a fine sieve and cool.

Oven temperature 375°F.

Make the strudel filling: Working with one pear at a time, peel and quarter it, then carefully remove the thin stem and core and slice into 1/2-inch chunks (this process should yield about 4 cups). Transfer the chunks to a stainless bowl and toss with a little lemon juice to prevent discoloration. When you have tossed the last pear chunks with lemon juice, fold in the currants and then sprinkle the flour, sugar, and allspice over the mixture. Gently toss together until the pears are evenly coated.

Clarify the butter: Melt the butter, and then bring it to a boil in a small saucepan over medium-low heat or in a glass dish for 30 seconds in the microwave—the butter will foam up when it begins to boil. Swirl it around in the pan for about 30 seconds until the foam subsides, then allow it to cool undisturbed for 4 to 5 minutes. Use a small ladle or spoon to skim the foam from the top, then tip the pan ever so gently. Carefully transfer the clear oil, ladleful by ladleful, to a small dish, leaving the milky sediment in the pan. Discard the sediment and blend the vegetable oil into the clarified butter.

Prepare the strudel: First, thaw the phyllo dough according to package directions.

Second, remove 8 phyllo sheets from the package and carefully lay them flat on a cool clean work surface. Immediately cover them with a damp paper towel or damp clean tea towel to keep them from drying out. (Note: As you work with the phyllo, be sure to remove only one sheet at a time from under the damp towel.)

Third, lay one sheet of phyllo on a cool clean surface and carefully brush it with a thin amount of the clarified butter. Lay a second sheet on top, brush it with butter and sprinkle it lightly with 1 tablespoon of the ground hazelnuts and 2 tablespoons of the fresh breadcrumbs. Repeat this process three times. (Do not sprinkle hazelnuts or crumbs over the top layer.)

Assemble the strudel: First, spoon the pear filling lengthwise in an even mound over the top sheet of phyllo, 3 inches from the bottom edge of the dough. Leave a 1-inch border at each end without any filling. Roll the 3-inch area of dough over the mounded filling and then continue to roll up the layers of dough into a cylinder. Flatten each end of the phyllo to seal in the filling. Liberally brush the outside with the remaining clarified butter and sprinkle with 1 tablespoon of sugar.

Second, use a long metal spatula to carefully transfer the strudel seam-side down to a lightly greased baking sheet. Use a sharp serrated knife to cut through the top layers of the dough in 2-inch intervals (or 6 equal portions). This will keep the strudel from breaking apart when you slice each portion. Bake until the dough is golden and the filling is just beginning to bubble, 35 to 40 minutes.

Serve the strudel: Carefully slice the strudel into portions using a serrated knife. Ladle a generous amount of sauce on each of 6 dessert plates, and place the strudel slices in the sauce. If desired, garnish each serving with additional pear slices, currants, and fresh mint leaves.

Easy Time-Saving and Do-Ahead Tips

SATURDAY:

- Prepare the vanilla sauce, cool to room temperature, and refrigerate.

- Prepare and cut the noodles; seal in plastic bags.

- Clean the chard, and peel and cut the kohlrabi; refrigerate in sealed plastic bags.

- Prepare the vegetables for the shanks.

SUNDAY MORNING:

- Braise the veal shanks.

- Prepare the strudel to the point of baking and refrigerate.

Chapter 14

AUTUMN *in* NEW ENGLAND

BUTTERNUT SQUASH *and* RUTABAGA MASH

OYSTERS *on the* HALF SHELL

SAGE-RUBBED ROAST PORK LOIN *with*
CRANBERRY-APPLE CIDER GLAZE

APPLE-RAISIN BREAD STUFFING

VERMONT MAPLE-WALNUT TART

I always feel at home in New England. It doesn't seem to matter which time of year. But perhaps my favorite time is during the autumn months. The cooling autumn weather brings with it the turning of the leaves—the colors of fall are bright red, reddish-brown, and deep green turned to rusty gold. I love the smell of the fallen leaves. I love the tranquil drive up winding roads, across the small and covered bridges, through the farmland and woods, where the skyline and woods are pierced with those signature white New England steeples.

Six states—Connecticut, Maine, Massachusetts, New Hampshire, Rhode Island, and Vermont—make up official New England. Each has a distinct cultural identity. Each state is made up of small incorporated municipalities that are locally governed. The town hall meetings of New England showcase some of the most direct democratic representation in the United States. A history of Puritanism mixed with liberal and progressive ideals and an agrarian lifestyle mixed with cottage industry and industrialism make New England unique.

The influences are many: French and Native Americans who trapped and traded; the English who colonized and settled in; the Greek, Italian, and Portuguese families who brought their trades to the coastal fishing villages; and the Irish who came to the mills during the famine and industrial revolution. And while there is no single New England style of cooking, there are flavors we often attribute to this picturesque corner of the country— foods the rest of us think of as distinctly New England.

Maple syrup and an abundance of squash, cranberries, apples, and apple cider are notable products of New England. Lobsters, cod, and oysters are among the treasured coastal harvest. Dairy farms produce some of the country's most distinct and renowned cheeses. All bring a bounty to our table.

Sunday dinner doesn't begin when we sit down to the table. A pick-up football game or the big game on TV are every bit a part of any family day, and we want to make our guests feel at home when they arrive. So while the roast is roasting and we put the finishing touches on the main meal, it's nice to have a little something to nibble on. What could be a better way to greet our gathering guests when they arrive than with a selection of freshly shucked oysters or a cheese board worthy of a Vermonter?

BUTTERNUT SQUASH *and* RUTABAGA MASH

8 Servings ■ ▪ ■ ▪ ■ ▪ ■ ▪ ■ ▪ ■ ▪ ■ ▪ ■ ▪ ■ ▪ ■ ▪ ■ ▪ ■

Rutabagas, or "Swedish turnips," are thought to be a cross between turnips and cabbage. They have a spicy, slightly sweet flavor that is very much like a turnip. They are really wonderful and pair perfectly with any variety of winter squash or with citrus-infused roasted carrots.

1 medium butternut squash

2 medium rutabagas

1 tablespoon vegetable oil

1/2 cup (1 stick) butter, divided

3 tablespoons dark brown sugar

1 cup vegetable broth

1/8 teaspoon allspice

Salt to season

Oven temperature 325°F.

First, remove the seeds from the squash. Lightly coat the rutabagas and squash with vegetable oil. Place them on a baking sheet cut side down and roast for 70 to 80 minutes, or until they are firm but soft enough to be easily pierced with the tip of a knife.

Second, when the squash and rutabagas are cool enough to handle, peel away the skin and any charred edges. Cut the rutabagas and squash into chunks.

Third, melt 4 tablespoons of the butter in a skillet with the brown sugar. Add in the chunks of rutabagas and squash as the butter melts and toss together. Pour in the vegetable broth, add the allspice, cover, and simmer for 10 to 12 minutes.

Finally, mash the roasted squash and rutabagas with the remaining butter. Season to taste with salt.

OYSTERS *on the* HALF SHELL

Many people are surprised to learn there are only a few species of oysters. Eastern Oysters (Crassostrea Virginica) *range from the cold waters of Canada throughout the mid–Atlantic to the Southern coastal states and the Gulf of Mexico. What matters is location. Oysters get their distinctive flavors and delicate textures more from their environment than from any other factor. The difference in flavor depends on the water temperature, salinity levels, the tides, and the mix of nutrients they feed on. Oysters from colder waters are plump with a sweeter taste and delicate texture. Oysters from saltier waters have a cleaner sharper finish. Oysters from warmer brackish waters are meaty and have richer flavor. Among my favorites are the highly prized Malpeques from Prince Edward Island, the creamy Wellfleets from Connecticut, and the Blue Points from Long Island.*

Autumn is the season for oysters. The best way to sample oysters—whether from local waters or from around the world—is freshly shucked and served on the half–shell with a splash of sherry vinegar, lemon, or cocktail sauce.

First, scrub the oysters under cold running water using a stiff brush to remove any sand and mud. Then place the scrubbed oysters on a flat dish in the refrigerator. Remember, oysters live in salt or brackish water and they will clam up to protect themselves against the tap water and human handling. Refrigerating will help them to relax so you won't have to pry them open.

Second, use a protective kitchen glove. Place the oyster with the flat side up and hold it firmly on a flat surface. Hold an oyster knife firmly and place the tip into the hinged end of the oyster.

Jiggle the knife quickly as you push it in and then give it a quick half-turn to "pop" the back end and break the airtight seal. Then slide the blade around the edge of the shell so the two halves are separated enough to slip in the blade. Turn the blade at an upward angle and cut across the inside of the top shell to separate the muscle from the shell. Discard the top shell. Cradle the oyster to keep it level so none of the juices spill and carefully slice the edge of the knife through the bottom muscle. The oyster is now swimming free for you to enjoy. Allow 4 to 6 oysters per person.

SAGE-RUBBED ROAST PORK LOIN *with* CRANBERRY-APPLE CIDER GLAZE

8 Servings

The sweet-tart cider glaze is an excellent complement to this succulent and seasoned pork loin roast. The crisp apples and tangy cranberries, along with a hint of mustard and spice combined with the earthy aroma of sage, are poised to create memorable and lingering flavors.

PORK LOIN

1/2 tablespoon mustard seeds

1/2 tablespoon white peppercorns

2 tablespoons whole-grain mustard

1/4 cup fresh chopped sage

1 tablespoon vegetable oil

1 bone-in pork loin roast, 5 to 6 pounds

1 tablespoon coarse salt

CIDER GLAZE

2 sweet-tart apples

1 small sweet onion

2 cups apple cider

1/4 cup dark corn syrup

1 tablespoon prepared yellow mustard

1/2 cup packed brown sugar

1 tablespoon cider vinegar

Pinch of ground cloves

1 cup fresh cranberries

Prepare the pork loin: Crush the mustard seeds and peppercorns using a mortar and pestle or the bottom of a heavy skillet. Combine crushed seeds and peppercorns in a small mixing bowl with the mustard, sage, and vegetable oil. Blend into a paste. Rub the roast evenly with the mustard paste. Cover the seasoned roast with plastic wrap and refrigerate overnight or for up to 24 hours.

Make the cider glaze: First, core and slice the apples and thinly slice the onion. In a heavy-bottomed saucepan whisk together the apple cider, corn syrup, mustard, brown sugar, cider vinegar, and pinch of ground cloves. Place the saucepan over a burner set to medium heat. Add in the apples, cranberries, and onion slices.

Second, bring the mixture to a boil and reduce the heat to medium-low. Simmer the sauce until the apples and cranberries are fully cooked, about 25 minutes. Strain the mixture through a sieve into a small bowl. Press firmly on the solids with a rubber spatula to squeeze out all the savory juices and pulp from the apple and onion slices. Discard the bits of apple peel, cranberry skins, and onion that remain in the sieve.

Oven temperature 325°F.

Roast the pork loin: First, remove the seasoned roast from the refrigerator and allow it to sit at room temperature for about 30 minutes. Season with coarse salt.

Second, position one oven rack near the bottom of the oven and the second rack just above— leaving enough room for the roast to easily fit on the bottom rack. Place the roast, with the ribs pointing upward, in a shallow roasting pan. Place the pan into the oven, and allow the pork to cook until the internal temperature registers about 130°F on a meat thermometer, 2 to 2¼ hours.

Third, increase the oven temperature to 350°F. Baste the roast with a generous amount of cider glaze, using a pastry brush to apply the glaze over the roast's entire surface. Repeat this glazing process two or three times while continuing to roast the meat for an additional 30 minutes.

Fourth, when the roast is cooked to an internal temperature of 150°F, take it out of the oven. Carefully remove the roast from the pan and allow the meat to rest on a clean cutting board for 15 to 20 minutes. The temperature will rise by another 5 to 10 degrees, giving you a medium serving temperature of 160°F.

Fifth, place the roasting pan on top of a burner that is set to medium heat. Pour about ¼ cup of warm water into the roasting pan and use a whisk to scrape the bits of meat from the bottom. Whisk in any remaining cider glaze and blend it with the pan juices. Simmer for 2 to 3 minutes to reduce the liquid and fully incorporate the rich flavors.

To serve: Hold the rib closest to you to secure the roast and carefully slice between each bone to cut each portion. The bones will have a slight curve to them, so use them as your guide rather than trying to cut straight down. Pass the pan juices alongside in a gravy boat.

APPLE-RAISIN BREAD STUFFING

8 Servings ■

Serving apples with pork is a natural choice, whether it is in the form of applesauce, baked apples, or spiced apples; so is serving pork with stuffing. This savory stuffing combines the best of both.

3 medium apples

2 tablespoons butter

3/4 cup diced celery

3/4 cup diced onion

1/4 cup apple cider

6 cups day-old raisin bread, cubed

1 tablespoon fresh chopped parsley

1 teaspoon dry rubbed sage

2 teaspoons coarse salt

1/4 teaspoon white pepper

1 cup chicken broth

2 eggs, beaten

Oven temperature 325°F.

First, peel, core, and dice the apples. Heat the butter over medium heat in a small skillet until it is just melted and beginning to bubble. Add in the diced apples, celery, and onion, and sauté until the onion is soft and translucent, 2 to 3 minutes. Add in the cider, remove the skillet from heat, and cool to room temperature.

Second, combine the bread cubes with the sautéed apple mixture in a stainless mixing bowl. Add in the parsley, dry sage, salt, and white pepper, and toss. Add in the chicken broth, 1/4 cup at a time, until the stuffing is moist. Carefully mix in the beaten eggs.

Third, butter the inside of a ceramic casserole or baking dish. Spoon the stuffing mixture into the casserole, cover, and bake for 50 minutes. Uncover the stuffing, increase the oven temperature to 350°F, and bake for 20 minutes more.

VERMONT MAPLE-WALNUT TART

8 Servings

When the Algonquian Indians introduced maple syrup to the Puritans, I doubt they had something as incredible as this rich, buttery, nutty tart in mind. Maple syrup is harvested throughout eastern North America, but nowhere can better, sweeter maple syrup be found than in Vermont. Maple syrup is enjoyed in so many ways, and the addition of walnuts creates a truly heavenly dessert.

For this recipe you'll need one 10-inch fluted false-bottom tart pan.

BROWN SUGAR CRUST

1 1/4 cups all-purpose flour

1/4 cup packed light brown sugar

1/2 teaspoon salt

1/4 cup (1/2 stick) unsalted butter

1 large egg yolk, room temperature

1 teaspoon pure vanilla extract

2 tablespoons whole milk, cold

MAPLE-WALNUT FILLING

1/4 cup (1/2 stick) unsalted butter, softened

1 cup packed dark brown sugar

3 large eggs, room temperature

1 cup pure Vermont maple syrup

1 teaspoon pure vanilla extract

1/2 teaspoon salt

2 cups chopped walnuts

Oven temperature 400°F.

Make the crust: First, combine the flour, brown sugar, and salt. Cut the butter into pieces and add to the flour mixture. Use a pasty cutter or a food processor fitted with a steel blade to cut in the butter until the mixture resembles coarse crumbly meal. Then add in the egg yolk, vanilla, and a sparse tablespoon of cold milk; mix long enough for the dough to just hold together. Add a few extra drops of milk as needed for the dough to reach the consistency of cookie dough. Roll into a ball, flatten into a disk, and wrap in plastic. Chill the dough in the refrigerator for at least 20 minutes and up to 5 days.

Second, on a clean dry surface that has been lightly dusted with a little granulated sugar, roll out the chilled tart dough into a 12-inch round. Carefully transfer the dough to the tart pan and gently press it into the corners, leaving about a 1/4-inch overhang. Fold the edges of the dough

inward and press firmly into the fluted pan so that the double edge extends about 1/8-inch above the rim. Place the tart shell in the freezer for 20 minutes.

Prepare the filling: First, cream the butter and brown sugar together in a mixing bowl. Whisk in the eggs until they are well blended. Beat in the maple syrup, vanilla, and salt.

Second, scatter the walnut pieces evenly over the bottom of the unbaked tart shell and pour in the filling. Place the tart on a baking sheet and bake for 10 minutes. Reduce the oven temperature to 350°F and continue baking until the filling is set, 30 to 40 more minutes. Remove from the oven and cool the tart to room temperature. If desired, serve topped with vanilla ice cream and warm maple syrup.

Easy Time-Saving and Do-Ahead Tips

SATURDAY:

- *Prepare the tart dough. Bake the tart, cool, and store at room temperature.*

- *Season the pork loin and refrigerate.*

SUNDAY MORNING:

- *Prepare the stuffing and the glaze.*

Chapter 15

TRAVELIN' THROUGH

STEAMED CAROLINA RICE

CHICKEN *and* SAUSAGE GUMBO

BAKED FLOUNDER *with* CRAB
STUFFING *and* REMOULADE SAUCE

DOUBLE SKILLET CORNBREAD

HOPPIN' JOHN

LEMON 'N' LIME MERINGUE PIE

I love traveling through the Southern coastal plains—from the Mississippi Delta along the Gulf of Mexico to the southern Atlantic coast and up through the low country of South Carolina—through the backwoods, waterways, marshes, and lowlands some call Hurricane Alley. The pace of life here is slow, like the tides and rivers that ebb and flow. And the foods are truly special; they are spicy yet subtle and always richly flavored.

The culinary influences are many: African, Creole, Spanish, French, Caribbean, and English. Each micro region is distinct, yet all share familiar ingredients and cooking styles. From Charleston to Savannah to Mobile and New Orleans—and countless points in between—you'll be served chunky, spicy gumbos, golden cornbread, and an array of fresh fish. You'll also come across dishes with curious names such as She-crab Soup, Limpin' Susan, Frogmore Stew, Shrimp Bog, and Hoppin' John. You'll find an abundance of succulent ingredients harvested from the wetlands: shrimp, crab, duck, oysters, and crawfish. And there's rice—always rice—the quintessential lowland grain. (You'll eat gumbo with rice, red beans and rice, dirty rice, rice with gravy, and rice pudding.) For dessert there are sweet, gooey delicacies such as pecan pie, blackberry cobbler, Key lime or lemon pie, and bread pudding.

Despite the natural abundance of these regions, poverty has also been a familiar companion in the lowland South. The people here learned long ago, however, that poverty of worldly wealth does not necessarily mean poverty of soul. That's why Sunday is more than just tradition. The day of rest always takes on greater meaning in a world born of struggle.

I love the style of preaching in so many lowland churches. It's poetic. I especially love gospel music, with its deep roots in rhythmic folk songs and field hollers. These are work songs, sorrow songs, and songs of faith in the face of hardship. They tell the story of poverty, slavery, misunderstanding, and injustice. They offer strength for trials and hope for the future. And though they remind us, again and again, that this world is not really our home, that all of us are really just traveling through, they also remind us of the wonderful truth that shines behind every Sunday: that even in this "vale of tears," we don't have to travel alone.

A long-held custom is for folks to gather with friend and family for fellowship after church where everyone brings something to the table. This buffet menu is perfect for such a celebration.

STEAMED CAROLINA RICE

8 Servings ■ ■■ ■ ■ ■■ ■ ■ ■ ■ ■ ■■ ■ ■ ■ ■ ■ ■■ ■ ■■ ■

Rice has long been a staple of Southern cooking and was once the foundation of the Southern economy. Rice should be fluffy—never sticky—where each grain is distinct. Converted rice is an excellent choice, but I like using any of the available heirloom varieties. Rice is best kept simple. Cooking rice is as easy as 1, 2, 3—1 cup rice, plus 2 cups liquid, equals 3 cups of cooked rice. Remember this simple formula, and you will never have to guess how much rice to make again. I like to use half chicken broth and half water without adding any additional salt. The butter brings out the sweetness of the rice and keeps the grains from sticking together.

4 cups water

2 cups chicken broth

3 cups rice

4 tablespoons unsalted butter

Rinse the rice 2 or three times under cold water to remove the excess starch. Pour the chicken broth and water into a 4-quart saucepan. Bring to a boil over high heat and add in the butter. Stir in the rice, reduce the heat to low, cover the pan with a tight-fitting lid, and continue cooking for 25 minutes. Turn off the heat and let the rice stand for an additional 10 minutes. (Do not lift the lid.)

To serve: Gently toss the rice with a fork. Garnish, if desired, with chopped green onions and parsley.

CHICKEN *and* SAUSAGE GUMBO

8 Servings ▪▪▪▪▪▪▪▪▪▪▪▪▪▪▪▪▪▪▪▪▪▪▪▪▪▪▪▪▪▪

From Louisiana to the Carolina coast, gumbo—big chunks of spicy goodness—is usually served as a main dish over rice. Today, it is often served as a first course soup. Many different types of meat and seafood are used in gumbo, including duck, chicken, and shrimp. Gumbo can be thickened using a dark roux, though it is often thickened and flavored just with the powdered young leaves of sassafras called filé powder.

4 boneless, skinless chicken thighs

1/2 teaspoon cayenne pepper

I teaspoon granulated garlic

I teaspoon onion powder

I teaspoon ground thyme

2 teaspoons salt

2 teaspoons pepper

6 tablespoons olive oil, divided

I cup diced green bell pepper

I cup diced celery

I cup diced onion

3 tablespoons all-purpose flour

2 tablespoons filé powder

4 cups chicken broth

I cup sliced okra

6 ounces sliced Andouille sausage

Salt to taste

1/4 to 1/2 teaspoon Tabasco sauce

1/2 cup sliced green onions

First, cut the chicken into chunks.

Second, whisk together the cayenne, garlic, onion powder, thyme, salt, and pepper in a medium mixing bowl. Place the chicken in the bowl and mix the seasoning thoroughly with the chunks of chicken. Cover and refrigerate for at least 4 hours and up to 24 hours.

Third, heat 4 tablespoons of the olive oil in a heavy-bottomed skillet over medium-high heat. Add the seasoned chicken to the skillet and sauté in the hot oil until the chicken is browned, 6 to 8 minutes. Use a slotted spoon to transfer the chicken from the skillet into a dish to cool.

Fourth, pour in the remaining 2 tablespoons of olive oil, reduce the heat to medium, and add in the bell pepper, celery, and onion. Sauté for 2 to 3 minutes.

Fifth, make a well in the center of the pan by pushing the vegetables to the edges; then tip the pan from side to side so most of the oil flows into

the center. Sprinkle the flour into the well—it will immediately begin to absorb some of the oil. Reduce the heat to medium-low and let the flour cook undisturbed for 4 to 5 minutes, then scrape the bottom of the skillet. (This will allow the flour to brown evenly.) Leave it to cook undisturbed for another 4 to 5 minutes.

Meanwhile, blend the filé into the chicken broth in a medium bowl.

Sixth, when the flour turns a deep even brown, stir it together with the vegetables and oil around the edges of the pan. Add in the okra, sausage, and cooked chicken with all of its juices. Stir together and cook for 2 minutes more.

Seventh, pour in the chicken broth. Bring to a boil, reduce the heat to low, and simmer for about 40 minutes, stirring from time to time until the okra is fully cooked and beginning to fall apart. Season the gumbo to taste with salt and Tabasco sauce. Garnish with green onions.

BAKED FLOUNDER *with* CRAB STUFFING *and* REMOULADE SAUCE

8 Servings

Stuffed fish is a wonderful Sunday treat. In the low coastal plains, delicate flatfish such as flounder are often stuffed with shrimp, crayfish, or crab. Blue crabs are what you find in the Southeast—when steamed, the sweet, succulent lump meat makes wonderful crab cakes, while the flaky back fin is used for stuffing and soups. Dungeness crabmeat is a good alternative, and you can stuff catfish, sole, or redfish fillets if you like.

REMOULADE SAUCE

1 cup mayonnaise

2 tablespoons fresh lemon juice

3 tablespoons minced onion

3 tablespoons minced sweet pickles

3 tablespoons fresh chopped parsley

1 teaspoon paprika

Pinch of cayenne pepper

2 to 3 drops Worcestershire sauce

Pinch of salt

STUFFING

1/4 cup (1/2 stick) butter

1/3 cup diced green bell pepper

1/3 cup diced celery

1/3 cup diced onion

1 pound steamed crabmeat

2 tablespoons all-purpose flour

1 cup fish stock or clam juice

1/4 teaspoon cayenne pepper

1 teaspoon dry mustard

1 teaspoon paprika

1/2 teaspoon celery salt

1 teaspoon Worcestershire sauce

4 or 5 drops Tabasco sauce

1/4 cup chopped green onions

2 tablespoons fresh chopped parsley

2 cups fresh breadcrumbs

FLOUNDER

8 (5- to 6-ounce) skinless fillets

Salt for seasoning

1/2 cup (1 stick) butter

2 lemons, halved

1 teaspoon paprika

2 tablespoons chopped green onions

1 tablespoon fresh chopped parsley

Make the Remoulade sauce: Whisk the mayonnaise together with the lemon juice in a small stainless mixing bowl. Fold in the minced onion, sweet pickles, and parsley. Season with the paprika, cayenne, Worcestershire sauce, and a pinch of salt. Cover and refrigerate for 4 hours or overnight to allow the flavors to meld.

Make the stuffing: First, melt the butter in a large skillet over medium heat. Add in the bell pepper, celery, and onion. Sauté until the vegetables are soft, 2 to 3 minutes. Add in the crabmeat and toss lightly with the vegetables; then sprinkle the flour into the pan and blend with the crab mixture to form a paste. Cook together for 2 to 3 minutes, stirring gently.

Second, pour in the fish stock or clam juice and stir until thick and bubbly. Season with the cayenne, dry mustard, paprika, and celery salt. Add the Worcestershire sauce and Tabasco sauce and remove the pan from the heat. Fold in the green onions, parsley, and breadcrumbs and allow to cool to room temperature.

Oven temperature 350°F.

Prepare the flounder: First, butter a large glass or ceramic dish. Divide the cooled stuffing into 8 equal mounds and place the mounds a couple of inches apart in the casserole so the fish fillets will not touch one another. Place 1 flounder fillet (or 2 smaller ones, if larger fish are unavailable) on top of each mound, skinned side up, and press gently.

Second, sprinkle the fillets with a little salt and dot the top of each with a tablespoon of butter. Juice the 2 lemons over the top and then lightly dust with paprika. Bake for 20 to 25 minutes.

Serve the flounder: Transfer the fillets to a warm platter. Sprinkle with the chopped green onions and parsley, and pour the pan juices over the top. If desired, garnish with fresh lemon slices. Serve the Remoulade on the side.

DOUBLE SKILLET CORNBREAD

Cornbread was baked in skillets long before most people had ovens. For those who didn't have a skillet, it was baked directly on the hearth or even cooked on the blade of a hoe out in the fields. Cornbread was traveling bread—what New Englanders called "journey" or "johnnycake" and Southern folks called "pone" or "hoecake."

2 cups yellow cornmeal

1 1/2 cups all-purpose flour

1/4 cup granulated sugar

1 tablespoon baking powder

2 teaspoons salt

3 large eggs, room temperature

2/3 cup whole milk

1 (8-ounce) can cream-style corn

1/4 cup (1/2 stick) unsalted butter

1/4 cup bacon fat or lard

Oven temperature 400°F.

First, combine the cornmeal, flour, sugar, baking powder, and salt in the bowl of a mixer fitted with a paddle; whisk together thoroughly. In a small bowl lightly beat the eggs into the milk. Add the egg mixture into the dry ingredients and mix together on low speed to form a smooth paste. Mix in the cream-style corn until just blended.

Second, heat a 10-inch heavy-bottomed or cast-iron skillet over medium heat. Add in the butter and the fat and allow it to bubble. Pour all but about 2 tablespoons of the melted bacon fat or lard into the cornbread batter and stir to combine thoroughly. Return the skillet to the stove. When the butter just begins to brown, pour the batter in the skillet. Let the cornbread cook on top of the stove just long enough for the fat to absorb into the batter, about 2 minutes. Gently shake the skillet back and forth to keep the batter from sticking to the bottom.

Third, transfer the skillet to the oven and bake, about 25 minutes until a wooden pick comes out clean when inserted into the center.

HOPPIN' JOHN

8 Servings

Numerous clever stories on how Hoppin' John got its name abound, such as young children hopping around the table in anticipation of this wonderfully simple dish or a hearty welcome call for dinner guests to "hop on in" and enjoy the food before them. More likely it is derived from the Creole pois a pigeon *(pwah-ah peejon), or pigeon peas, that are enjoyed throughout the Caribbean.*

Many Hoppin' John recipes call for the black-eyed peas to be combined with rice; others do not. I prefer to keep the peas as a separate dish which can then be spooned over rice or crumbled cornbread. This traditional Southern recipe, with the contrasting sweet tomatoes and briny country ham, offers a perfect complement to the smoky, earthy black-eyed peas.

I cup dried black-eyed peas

I tablespoon peanut oil

4 ounces country ham, diced

1/2 cup diced onion

2 cups water

1/2 cup diced celery

1/4 cup diced green bell pepper

I (15-ounce) can stewed tomatoes

I teaspoon salt

1/4 teaspoon black pepper

1/8 teaspoon ground cayenne pepper

Pinch of allspice

First, pick through the black-eyed peas and rinse them thoroughly. Soak the peas for 8 hours or overnight in 1 quart of cold water. Drain and set aside.

Second, heat the peanut oil in a heavy pot over medium-high heat and brown the ham. Reduce the heat to medium, add the diced onion, and sauté until translucent, 2 to 3 minutes. Add the black-eyed peas, stir together, and pour in the water to cover the peas. Bring to a boil, reduce the heat to low, cover with a tight-fitting lid and simmer until the peas are tender, about 45 minutes. Add the diced celery, bell pepper, tomatoes, salt, black pepper, red pepper, and allspice, and stir to combine. Simmer, uncovered, for an additional 15 to 20 minutes or until the peas are tender.

Serve as a side dish or spooned over rice and with hot pepper sauce.

LEMON 'N' LIME MERINGUE PIE

8 Servings ■

I love lemon meringue pie, and I really love this lemon 'n' lime pie. Lemon pies can often be too sweet or too slight on that fresh lemon flavor . . . here's a recipe that has true lemon–lime flavor with a light meringue and an easy crust made with zesty gingersnaps. It is a prized recipe, worthy of a Junior League bake sale or church supper dessert.

PIE CRUST

1 (8-ounce) package gingersnaps

1/4 cup granulated sugar

5 tablespoons unsalted butter, melted

FILLING

1 1/2 cups granulated sugar

5 tablespoons cornstarch

Pinch of salt

1 1/2 cups lemon-lime soda

1/3 cup fresh lemon juice

1/3 cup fresh lime juice

Zest of 1 lemon

Zest of 1 lime

1/2 tablespoon unflavored gelatin

2 tablespoons cold water

4 egg yolks, room temperature

3 tablespoons unsalted butter

MERINGUE

4 egg whites, room temperature

1/4 teaspoon cream of tartar

8 tablespoons superfine sugar, divided

Oven temperature 400°F.

Prepare the crust: Combine the gingersnaps and the sugar in the bowl of a food processor fitted with a steel blade. Pulse until you have fine crumbs; then pour in the melted butter and pulse until thoroughly combined. Press the mixture into the bottom and up the sides of a 1-inch-deep pie dish. Bake until brown, 8 to 10 minutes. Cool.

Make the filling: First, combine the sugar, cornstarch, and salt with the lemon-lime soda in a 2-quart heavy-bottomed saucepan and whisk together until smooth. Cook over medium heat, stirring constantly, until the mixture begins to boil. Then immediately turn the heat to low and add in the lemon juice, lime juice, lemon zest, and lime zest. Continue cooking until bubbles begin to break over the entire surface, 2 to 3 minutes more.

Meanwhile, sprinkle the gelatin over the water and let stand for 4 to 5 minutes, and then stir to dissolve.

Second, lightly whisk the egg yolks in a medium mixing bowl. Add about 1/2 cup of the hot lemon filling to the egg yolks to temper them, whisk in the dissolved gelatin until smooth and then slowly blend the tempered yolks back into the lemon mixture. Stir over low heat for about 2 minutes. Remove the pan from the heat to cool. After 3 to 4 minutes, stir in the butter a tablespoon at a time. Cool uncovered for 5 minutes.

Third, pour the hot filling into the baked pie shell. To keep a skin from forming, cover the top with a piece of waxed paper that has been brushed with a little melted butter. Cool the pie to room temperature and then refrigerate until just a couple of hours before you plan to serve—wait until then to top the pie with the meringue.

Prepare the meringue: Beat the egg whites until foamy in the bowl of a mixer fitted with a clean dry whisk. Add in the cream of tartar and 4 tablespoons of the superfine sugar and beat until stiff peaks form. Gently fold in the remaining 4 tablespoons of superfine sugar.

Assemble the pie: Remove the waxed paper from the surface of the lemon-lime filling. Use a pastry bag to pipe rosettes of meringue over the surface of the pie, or spoon the meringue over the pie and create peaks using a spatula or pastry knife. Be sure to spread the meringue so that it seals the entire edge of the crust to keep the meringue from shrinking as it bakes. Bake until golden and set, about 12 minutes. Cool the meringue by placing the pie on an open rack in the freezer for 10 to 15 minutes. Keep the pie refrigerated until 10 to 15 minutes before serving, at which point you can let it rest at room temperature.

Easy Time-Saving and Do-Ahead Tips

SATURDAY:

- Prepare the crab stuffing and the Remoulade sauce; cover and refrigerate.
- Bake the pie crust and fill with the lemon filling; cover and refrigerate.
- Prepare the soup and chill.
- Soak the black-eyed peas.
- Measure out the dry ingredients for the cornbread.

SUNDAY MORNING:

- Top the pie with meringue and bake.
- Stuff the fish, place in the baking dish, cover with plastic, and refrigerate.
- Prepare the Hoppin' John.

ONE HOUR BEFORE DINNER:

- Bake the cornbread.
- Finish preparing the gumbo.

Chapter 16

WHEN YOU'RE FAMILY

RIGATONI PASTA *with* BRAISED BEEF
and ITALIAN SAUSAGE RAGU

CHOPPED TRATTORIA SALAD
with ROMANO VINAIGRETTE

CHOCOLATE-ESPRESSO TORTONI

When you're family, there's always a place at the table. When you're family, you're welcome to stay the night. When you're family, you don't need a reservation (although it's nice if you phone ahead!). For Americans of Italian heritage, Sunday has long been a treasured family day, begun in the warmth and bustle of the kitchen in the morning and continued around the great table after church, with good food and lively conversation lingering on until the evening.

Italian-Americans make up the fourth largest ethnic group in our country. The largest influx of Italians arrived in the East between 1880 and the 1920s. The economic conditions, much of it caused by Italian unification in the mid-nineteenth century, were particularly hard on southern Italy and Sicily. Many came alone or as father and son, without their families and crowded into steerage. Often families would scrape together enough money for one ticket, hoping the chosen one would prosper and help the rest come to the new country as well.

Others came to California during the Gold Rush. Many of San Francisco's earliest settlers came from northern Italy, from Liguria to Veneto. They brought to the city a love of opera, that famous sourdough bread, and, equally famous, Ghirardelli chocolate. They also made good use of a Mediterranean climate and coast rich in seafood—not unlike the one at home—to create dishes such as cioppino and to transform a fledgling wine industry. Together Italian-Americans changed the way America eats and brought foods that have become American classics.

Italian cooking has always been a true fusion cuisine, combining foods and cooking styles from many lands—Egyptian wheat, Chinese pasta, Arabian flatbread, Indian eggplant and rice, and tomatoes, peppers, and corn from the New World—into a distinct collection of regional flavors. (There are twenty regions of Italy, each with its own cooking style.) Each region, like each family, believes their food style and dishes are the most authentic.

No matter where one's family is from and no matter which style one favors, Italian is still Italian. And despite differences, most will say that family is still family, linked by blood, tradition, culture, and faith. Gathered together we touch past, present, and future; around the common table we celebrate our common bonds. Surely this is the essence of Sunday dinner.

RIGATONI PASTA *with* BRAISED BEEF *and* ITALIAN SAUSAGE RAGU

10 Servings

One mid-Atlantic culinary tradition is "Sunday Gravy." Sunday Gravy is marinara sauce, where a variety of meats—veal or pork shoulder, neck bones, short ribs, oxtails, or chuck roast—are braised together with Italian sausage to give the classic tomato sauce a rich meaty flavor. Some families serve the meats separately. Others simmer everything into a meaty stew. Whether you call it Sunday gravy or Ragu doesn't really matter—it's quite a dish! I prefer to use bulk sausage broken into chunks; others like to cook the sausage whole and slice the links into pieces to simmer in the sauce. Your favorite meatballs make an excellent addition as well.

RAGU

1 pound beef chuck, cut into 1-inch pieces

Coarse salt and cracked pepper

1/3 cup extra virgin olive oil, divided

2 cups red wine, divided

1 pound sweet Italian sausage

10 cloves garlic, sliced

1 medium onion, diced

1 (28-ounce) can crushed tomatoes

1 (28-ounce) can whole plum tomatoes

1 (8-ounce) package fresh mushrooms, quartered

4 tablespoons tomato paste

2 tablespoons dried basil leaves

2 cups water

2 tablespoons fresh chopped basil

2 tablespoons fresh chopped Italian parsley

PASTA

1 pound dried Rigatoni pasta

Prepare the ragu: First, season the beef with salt and pepper. Heat just enough olive oil to lightly coat the bottom of a large skillet. When the oil is hot, reduce the temperature to medium, add the meat, and brown it slowly, turning every minute or so. When the meat is evenly browned on all sides, deglaze the pan with 1/3 cup of the red wine. Simmer for 3 to 4 minutes and remove the pan from the heat.

Second, use the same skillet and heat just enough of the olive oil to coat the bottom. (If you are using link sausage, remove and discard the casings.) Break the sausage into bite-size pieces and brown over medium-high heat.

Third, when the sausage is browned, push the pieces to the edges of the skillet. Pour the remaining olive oil into the center of the skillet and heat for a minute or so. Add the garlic and onion, and sauté over medium heat until translucent, 2 to 3 minutes.

Fourth, pour the crushed tomatoes into the skillet. Use a wooden spoon to mix in the sausage, garlic, and onions. Stir until the olive oil and the crushed tomatoes are fully combined. Empty the can of whole tomatoes into a bowl Use your hands to gently break the tomatoes into pieces and add them to the skillet. Increase the heat to high, pour in the remaining red wine, and blend into the tomato sauce. Allow the sauce to bubble for 2 to 3 minutes to cook off the alcohol, stirring as it cooks. Whisk in the tomato paste, add in the browned beef, mushrooms, and basil leaves. Mix in the water. Simmer over low heat, stirring from time to time, for 2 hours, or until the pieces of beef are tender enough to shred with a fork and the ragu is thickened.

Finally, season to taste with salt and pepper, and add in the fresh chopped basil and parsley.

Prepare the pasta: Bring 4 quarts of salted water, with 2 tablespoons olive oil, to a boil in a large pot. Add the pasta and cook until al dente, about 10 minutes. Quickly drain the cooked pasta in a colander, toss gentle to remove any excess water, and transfer to a large serving bowl. Toss the ragu with the pasta. Serve immediately with grated cheese.

CHOPPED TRATTORIA SALAD
with ROMANO VINAIGRETTE

10 Servings

It seems every Trattoria around serves a similar house salad. Crisp lettuces chopped and chocked full of peppers, olives, onions, and a simple dressing. Add what you want to make the salad your own: marinated artichoke hearts, garbanzo beans, fresh tomatoes, or zucchini are nice additions. A favorite of mine are avocados—perhaps because I grew up in California where we had an avocado tree in our back yard.

SALAD

1 medium head iceberg lettuce

2 heads romaine hearts

1 head radicchio

1 (12-ounce) jar cracked green olives

1 (12-ounce jar) pepperoncini peppers

1 medium cucumber, sliced

1 small red onion, sliced thin

DRESSING

2 whole cloves garlic

1/3 cup white wine vinegar

2/3 cup extra virgin olive oil

1 teaspoon coarse salt

1/2 teaspoon coarse-ground black pepper

1/4 teaspoon red pepper flakes

1 tablespoon fresh chopped oregano

1/4 cup grated Romano cheese

Make the salad: Thoroughly rinse the lettuces in cold water to refresh them. Discard any tough stems or wilted leaves. Chop the iceberg, romaine, and radicchio into bite-size pieces. Dry in a colander covered with a clean tea towel or in a salad spinner. Pitt the olives and cut in half. Remove the stems and seeds from the peppers and cut in half. Toss the lettuces with the sliced olives, peppers, sliced cucumber, and onion. Refrigerate in a salad bowl covered with a damp paper towel or plastic wrap until you are ready to serve.

Prepare the dressing: Finely grate the garlic cloves into a small mixing bowl. Whisk in the vinegar, and then slowly whisk in the extra virgin olive oil until blended. Add the salt, black pepper, red pepper flakes, oregano, and Romano cheese, and whisk until blended.

Just before serving, lightly toss the salad with the dressing.

CHOCOLATE-ESPRESSO TORTONI

10 Servings

Italy is renowned for its desserts, and there are many kinds of light and airy frozen and refrigerated desserts to choose from—Spumoni, Gelato, Cassata, and Tortoni are among them. Tortoni is generally attributed to Giuseppe Tortoni, who made the frozen concoction chocked full of candied cherries and toasted almonds at his Paris café. A more traditional recipe calls for beaten egg whites, but with health concerns over raw eggs, that is not recommended.

3 egg yolks

1/2 cup granulated sugar

1/2 cup strong brewed coffee

1 pint premium coffee ice cream

1 1/2 cups heavy cream, stiffly whipped

1/2 cup grated bittersweet chocolate

1/2 cup crushed Italian almond cookies

1 teaspoon ground espresso coffee

First, combine the egg yolks, sugar, and brewed coffee in a stainless bowl. Place over a pan of simmering water and whisk the mixture until it is thick and fluffy, 3 to 4 minutes. Place over a pan of cold water and continue beating until chilled.

Second, soften the ice cream and combine with the chilled yolk mixture. Fold in the whipped cream and then the grated chocolate, crushed cookies, and ground espresso. Quickly, divide between ten chilled 8-ounce custard or coffee cups. Seal with plastic wrap and freeze for 4 hours.

To serve, if the Tortoni are frozen solid, remove them from the freezer and place them in the refrigerator about 1 hour before serving. Top with a dollop of freshly whipped cream, and garnish with shaved chocolate and chocolate espresso beans or Maraschino cherries. Serve with almond cookies.

Easy Time-Saving and Do-Ahead Tips

SATURDAY:

- Prepare the ragu.
- Prepare and freeze the Tortoni.
- Prepare the salad dressing.

SUNDAY MORNING:

- Prepare the salad ingredients and refrigerate in sealed containers.

Chapter 17

A HOMESPUN GATHERING

GRANDMA'S FRIED CHICKEN

GARLIC-HERB MASHED POTATOES

DILLY SUMMER SQUASH SAUTÉ

FRIED GREEN TOMATOES

FROZEN VANILLA CUSTARD

WARM PEACH COBBLER

When I was young, my family would often visit my father's parents, who owned a general store out in the high desert of Southern California—at the crossroads of Kern County, where the southern end of the vast California Central Valley rises along the edges of the Sierra Nevada mountains. Grandma Cronkhite always made fried chicken for Sunday dinner, and she always fried up just drumsticks—a treat for us kids because we could eat with our fingers and it was easy to dip the chicken into the mashed potatoes and gravy. My grandpa used to tell us that the platters of drumsticks came from twelve-legged chickens—he called them "desert chickens." No matter how many times he told us the same story, we'd laugh as though we'd never heard it before.

To get there, we'd leave early in the morning just after breakfast to avoid driving through the blistering heat of the noonday sun—my mom, my two sisters, my older brother, and I. The girls would be in their bright dresses, we boys in our pressed summer shorts and matching shirts. It always seemed to be a sunny day, so Mom usually had the top down as we made the long run out of the city.

Down the highways and country roads; past the endless cotton fields, ranch lands, and orange groves; and through the small towns we'd roll. I loved the smell of the eucalyptus trees and bay laurels fragrant in the morning sun. I remember the vast oil fields with those pumps slowly groaning up and down, up and down, like giant mechanical dinosaurs—relics of another age.

Grandma and Grandpa would always greet us with hugs outside between the car and the porch, holding us just long enough before my brother and I raced inside for a cold drink. Mom always scolded us about not asking first and to not ruin our dinner by filling up on soda—I don't recall we ever did.

The store was closed on Sunday, but Grandpa always seemed to have it open anyway. Not for locals, but for those like us passing through on a Sunday drive. "Folks have to get gas somewhere" he reckoned—gas and something cool to wet their thirst —especially in the summer. The store's shelves and bins were a ramshackle of local produce, household items, and homespun wares—products still found at local weekend farmer's markets.

Grandma's table was always set with checkered cloth. And while we might enjoy a soda beforehand, dinner was always served with ice-cold milk poured from a pitcher. As the afternoon wore on, games and conversations would turn to a cool evening and we'd all wave good-bye until another Sunday of fried chicken legs and the homespun stories that make up so much of our family lore.

GRANDMA'S FRIED CHICKEN

8 to 10 Servings ■

You could start a war over fried chicken—bathed in buttermilk, brined, spicy, not spicy, seasoning first and flour second, this temperature or that. We all have our favorites, and this is mine. Like Grandma Cronkhite, I like to keep it simple!

FRIED CHICKEN

2 frying chickens, 3 $1/2$ pounds each

1 cup all-purpose flour

1 teaspoon granulated garlic

2 teaspoons onion powder

1 tablespoon combined fresh chopped herbs; parsley, sage, and thyme

2 teaspoons poultry seasoning

1 teaspoon ground black pepper

2 tablespoons salt

Vegetable shortening for frying

GRAVY

3 tablespoons pan drippings

3 tablespoons all-purpose flour

1 cup water

3 cups chicken broth

Salt and pepper to taste

Prepare the chicken: First, rinse the chickens thoroughly under cold running water and pat dry with paper towels. Use a sharp knife to cut each chicken into 8 pieces—breasts, thighs, legs, and wings (you may want to cut the larger breasts in half).

Second, whisk together the flour, granulated garlic, onion powder, fresh herbs, poultry seasoning, black pepper, and salt in a mixing bowl. One by one, dredge the pieces of chicken in the seasoned flour until they are heavily coated, and lay the pieces out on a wire rack. Allow the chicken to sit for 10 minutes until the seasoned flour is becoming absorbed into the chicken. Redredge each piece 2 minutes before frying.

Third, place a large cast-iron or heavy-bottomed skillet over medium-high heat. Melt enough shortening to cover the bottom of the skillet, about $1/2$-inch deep. Heat the shortening until it reaches 325°F or until a pinch of flour sizzles when added.

Fry the chicken: First, drop the thighs, skin side down, into the center of the pan, followed by the legs, the breasts, and the wings. Adjust the heat to maintain an even temperature of 325°F. Fry the

About Fried Chicken

Fried chicken should be fully cooked to an internal temperature of 180°F so that the meat is moist and tender, and easily pulls away from the bones. Remember that a piece of white meat cooks more quickly, in about 1/4 less time, than an equal-sized piece of dark meat. As a result, white meat should be placed in the oil a few minutes after the dark meat, with the thighs in the middle. For a large batch you can cook the pieces separately.

The best temperature for pan-frying is around 325°F. Frying chicken slowly will allow the chicken to fully cook in the center while not browning too much on the outside. Use a large heavy skillet for even frying and to keep the chicken from scorching on the bottom. Do not overcrowd the pan.

Some traditional methods call for a tight-fitting lid to be placed on the skillet so that the chicken "steams" and the flavor permeates the meat—this is the basic idea behind our popular takeout brands that use pressure-fryers. I prefer this method, but since I also prefer crispy chicken and don't have a pressure-fryer, I simply remove the lid during the last 10 minutes of cooking.

Vegetable shortening is perfect for frying chicken. (Peanut oil and some vegetable oils have a stronger flavor.) You can strain and reuse the frying oil if kept refrigerated in an airtight container for up to sixty days.

chicken undisturbed for 5 minutes. Cover the skillet with a tight-fitting lid, and fry for an additional 10 minutes. Remove the lid and carefully turn the pieces over using a pair of tongs. Cover the skillet again for 5 minutes. Remove the lid and continue frying the chicken 10 to 12 minutes until the pieces are fully cooked to an internal temperature of 180°F and the juices run clear when tested with a knife. Place the fried chicken pieces on paper towels to blot the excess oil and transfer to a serving platter. (If you are making two batches, place the first batch on a wire rack set in a baking sheet and keep warm in a 250°F oven.) Reserve 1/4 cup of the oil for frying the tomatoes.

Make the gravy: Pour off all but 3 tablespoons of the oil through a sieve and return all of the crunchy seasoned bits caught by the sieve back into the skillet. Sprinkle 3 tablespoons of flour over the oil and whisk to form a paste or light roux. Slowly pour in the water, followed by the chicken broth, whisking constantly and scraping the brown meaty pieces from the bottom of the skillet, until the liquid blends with the paste to form the gravy. Let the gravy simmer for about 5 minutes; season to taste with salt and pepper.

GARLIC-HERB MASHED POTATOES

8 Servings ■■■■■■■■■■■■■■■■■■■■■■■■

I like to make mashed potatoes by replacing the salt with chicken bouillon cubes or concentrated chicken stock added to the water while cooking the potatoes, seasoned with a hint of garlic and fresh herbs. You can reduce the calories or dairy by replacing the milk in the recipe with 2/3 cup of the seasoned potato water and using a couple tablespoons of olive oil in place of the butter. These potatoes are also great with roasted chicken.

8 medium white potatoes

Cold water, as needed

1 small garlic clove, sliced thin

2 or 3 springs fresh thyme

2 chicken bouillon cubes or 2 tablespoons concentrated chicken stock

1/2 cup (1 stick) butter

2/3 cup whole milk

Salt and pepper to taste

First, peel the potatoes, pare away any eyes, and cut into quarters. Place the potatoes in a large pot filled with enough cool water to cover them completely. Add the garlic, thyme, and chicken bouillon or stock to the water. Heat the water to a low boil and simmer until the potatoes are completely cooked, 20 to 25 minutes.

Second, drain the seasoned water from the potatoes, leaving them in the pot. Return the pot to the stove and let them cook for about a minute, shaking the pan, to let the excess moisture evaporate. Add in the butter and continue to shake the pan until the butter melts completely and coats all of the potatoes (this will keep them from becoming sticky when they are mashed). Pour in the milk and bring to a boil. Remove the pan from the heat, and mash the potatoes until fluffy. Season to taste with salt and pepper.

DILLY SUMMER SQUASH SAUTÉ

8 Servings

I prefer to use tender little pattypan squash for this dish. If you can't find pattypan, use small crookneck or any variety of summer squash. If the squash are large, cut them in half lengthwise and use a spoon to scrape out the seeds and spongy centers, which tend to become bitter during cooking.

2 pounds tiny yellow squash

3 tablespoons butter

1 small sweet onion

Salt to season

2 tablespoons granulated sugar

1 tablespoon cider vinegar

1 tablespoon fresh chopped dill

Trim the ends from the squash and cut each squash in half. Heat the butter in a skillet over medium heat until the butter just begins to bubble. Cut the onion in half crosswise and then slice the halves into slivers. Add the onion slivers to the skillet and sauté until soft and translucent, about 2 minutes. Add the squash, season with salt, and sauté until the squash are tender, 3 to 4 minutes. Sprinkle the sugar over the squash, and add the vinegar. Toss in the dill, and cook for 1 minute more.

FRIED GREEN TOMATOES

8 Servings

Fried green tomatoes are a wonderful addition to any country-style menu and especially during late spring and early summer when tomatoes first appear on the vine. The trick is to fry them quickly for a crunchy outside and firm, just warm middle.

2 pounds firm green tomatoes

Flour for dredging

1 egg, beaten with 2 tablespoons water

1/2 cup dried breadcrumbs

1/4 cup shortening from the fried chicken

2 tablespoons butter

Cornmeal, as needed

Salt to season

Cut the tomatoes into 1/2-inch slices. Dredge in the flour, followed by the egg wash, and then the breadcrumbs. Heat the oil and butter in a skillet over medium-high heat. Fry the breaded tomato slices in the hot oil until brown, for 1 to 2 minutes per side. Place the fried tomato slices on paper towels to blot the excess oil and place on a sheet pan lightly coated in corn meal. Lightly season the tops with salt. Serve immediately.

FROZEN VANILLA CUSTARD

2 Quarts ▪▪▪▪▪▪▪▪▪▪▪▪▪▪▪▪▪▪▪▪▪▪▪▪▪▪▪▪▪▪

Just "plain" vanilla . . . ? I don't think so! It is the ratio of egg yolks to butterfat that turns ice cream into premium frozen custard. The key to rich frozen custard is to churn slowly so that little air is whipped into the mixture and to use just enough sugar to sweeten without overpowering the creamy vanilla flavor.

8 large egg yolks, room temperature

1 cup granulated sugar

1 vanilla bean

4 cups half-and-half

2 cups heavy cream

First, place the egg yolks in a stainless bowl or in the top of a double boiler. Slowly beat in the sugar with a wire whisk—it's important that the sugar dissolves slowly and completely into the yolks and that you do not beat the mixture too rapidly, which will make the yolks frothy and full of air.

Second, split the vanilla bean in half lengthwise and combine with the half-and-half in a saucepan. Heat slowly over medium heat until the half-and-half just begins to boil. Remove from the heat immediately.

Third, temper the yolks by whisking 1/2 cup of the hot half-and-half into the yolk mixture until fully blended. Whisk in the remaining hot half-and-half. Place the bowl over a pan of simmering water, making sure that the bowl does not touch the water. Cook the custard, stirring constantly with a heat-resistant rubber spatula, until thickened, 6 to 8 minutes. To test for thickness: Dip a spoon into the sauce and hold it horizontally over the pan, making sure that the sauce coats the spoon evenly. Then run your finger through the sauce on the back of the spoon—if the line doesn't fill back up, it has thickened enough.

Fourth, remove the vanilla bean and strain the custard through a fine sieve into a stainless bowl. Cool by partially submerging the bowl in a bowl of ice water. Stir gently until cool. Stir in the heavy cream, and scrape all of the tiny seeds from the vanilla bean into the custard. Whisk the custard thoroughly. Process the custard in an ice cream freezer according to the manufacturer's instructions.

WARM PEACH COBBLER

8 Servings ■ ▪ ▪ ▪ ▪ ▪ ▪ ■ ▪ ▪ ▪ ▪ ▪ ▪ ■ ▪ ▪ ▪ ▪

Peaches ripen slowly in the summer sun and grow juicy as the sap begins to sweeten. Few things are as satisfying as warm fruit cobbler topped with fresh homemade ice cream.

PEACH FILLING

8 cups fresh sliced peaches or frozen peaches, thawed

1 tablespoon fresh lemon juice

1 teaspoon ground cinnamon

Pinch of ground nutmeg or mace

3 tablespoons cornstarch

1/2 cup packed light brown sugar

1/2 cup granulated sugar

1/4 cup (1/2 stick) unsalted butter

COBBLER TOPPING

1 1/2 cups all-purpose flour

1 cup cake flour

4 teaspoons baking powder

1/2 teaspoon salt

8 tablespoons (1 stick) unsalted butter

1/3 cup granulated sugar

2 large eggs, room temperature, lightly beaten

3/4 cup whole milk

Oven temperature 375°F.

Make the filling: Combine the sliced peaches with the lemon juice, cinnamon, and nutmeg or mace in a large mixing bowl. Add the cornstarch, brown sugar, and granulated sugar, and toss together. Cut the butter into little pieces and add to the bowl. Transfer to a buttered 13 x 9-inch baking dish.

Make the topping: First, sift the all-purpose flour, cake flour, baking powder, and salt into a mixing bowl. Slice 8 tablespoons of butter into 1-inch pieces and scatter the pieces over the flour mixture. Sprinkle with the sugar, and cut all of the ingredients together with a pastry cutter until the mixture resembles coarse crumbly meal.

Second, whisk the eggs and milk together in a separate bowl, then add to the crumbly mixture. Stir with a wooden spoon until the dough just blends together and reaches the consistency of wet biscuit dough.

Third, spoon the topping into mounds over the peach filling. Brush the mounds with a little milk and sprinkle with a little granulated sugar. Bake until the topping is golden and the fruit is bubbling, 40 to 45 minutes.

Easy Time-Saving and Do-Ahead Tips

SATURDAY:

- Prepare the frozen custard.
- Trim the squash and store in a sealed container.

SUNDAY MORNING:

- Peel the potatoes and place in cold water.
- Mix the biscuit topping for the cobbler.
- Season the chicken.

Chapter 18

MOUNTAIN'S MAJESTY

CHILI-PECAN CRUSTED BROOK TROUT

FIELD GREENS, ROASTED BEETS, *and*
ONION SALAD *with* CREAMY GOAT
CHEESE *and* RASPBERRY VINAIGRETTE

ROSEMARY FINGERLING POTATOES

SKILLET CORN *and* PEPPERS

SWEET CHERRY-PLUM PANDOWDY

In 1893, Katherine Lee Bates stood atop 14,000-foot-tall Pike's Peak with a group of fellow professors summering in Colorado. Electrified by the majesty that lay before her, she wrote "America the Beautiful."

That same scene of mountain majesty has inspired me many times. For years my family lived high in the mountains of Colorado, surrounded by the Pike National Forest, where I worked as the chef for a guest ranch and a family retreat. Three of our four children were born in Colorado. We lived in, and around, the small Western towns with their wood-planked sidewalks, tack shops, general stores, and small cozy cafés.

What a spectacular place to live! In the summer we'd hike and picnic under the mountains' glorious gaze, and in the winter we'd ski the backwoods on never-touched white powder. We'd hunt and fish in some of the best places in the country. Indeed, some of my fondest memories are heading deep into the mountains to find that perfect stream—the headwaters of so many rivers—to seek the elusive native cut-throat or golden trout. Here, a 4 x 4 is a valuable tool and horses are a way of life. We'd camp in the remote outback. At night, the black velvet sky would twinkle with so many stars that we couldn't begin to count them—the wonders of creation.

My wife and I often attended worship services in a small country church that sat just on the edge of town. In the warmer months we'd gather out of doors in a great meadow beneath the aspen stands or beside a small lake that reflected the still-snowcapped peaks. Sunday dinner after church was always a multifamily affair, and everyone pitched in to help—from the oldest to the young. There would be fresh-caught trout and succulent meats from the wood-fired grill—brisket, chicken, and venison. Fresh roasted corn, an array of crisp garden salads, and homemade, orchard-picked fruit desserts—cobblers, pies, pandowdies and tarts—would round out the meal. After grace (when those ever-present cowboy hats would finally come off), the food-laden platters would make their way around great knotty-pine tables and we'd feast.

Colorado still holds fond memories for our family. It's not just the beautiful streams, peaceful meadows, and towering mountain peaks that cause our hearts to stir. Our deepest memories are of a particular place and the community life we shared with those who gave us so much more than Sunday afternoons.

CHILI-PECAN CRUSTED BROOK TROUT

6 Servings ▪▪▪▪▪▪▪▪▪▪▪▪▪▪▪▪▪▪▪▪▪▪▪▪▪

It's always nice to have freshly caught brook trout—their flesh is firm and pink and ever so succulent. Trout has a very delicate flavor and should not be overpowered. The buttermilk and hint of chili add a little zest and accent the cornmeal and pecans nicely. I find that using a large griddle pan works best for this and similar recipes.

2/3 **cup all-purpose flour**

2 **teaspoons red chili powder**

1 **teaspoon lemon pepper**

1 **teaspoon salt**

2 **large eggs, beaten**

3/4 **cup buttermilk**

1/2 **cup stone-ground cornmeal**

1 **cup finely ground pecans**

12 **fresh boneless, skin-on brook trout fillets**

2 **tablespoons safflower oil**

3 **tablespoons butter**

Lemon wedges, for garnish

First, set up a dredging station: In one dish place the flour whisked together with the chili powder, lemon pepper, and salt. In the second dish place the eggs, beaten together with the buttermilk. In the third dish combine the cornmeal with the pecans. Dredge the trout fillets in the seasoned flour, followed by the egg wash, and then the cornmeal-pecan mixture. Press each fillet firmly into the cornmeal and pecans for an even coating. Place the fillets on parchment or waxed paper.

Second, pour a tablespoon or so of oil onto a griddle set over medium-high heat. Evenly distribute 2 to 3 tablespoons of butter onto the griddle. When the butter begins to melt, place half of the fillets, skin side up, on the griddle and brown for 3 to 4 minutes. Carefully turn the fillets over and brown for 2 to 3 minutes more.

Third, place the fillets on paper towels to blot the excess oil, transfer them to a wire rack, and keep them warm in an oven. Repeat the process with the remaining fillets. Serve immediately, garnished with lemon wedges.

FIELD GREENS, ROASTED BEETS, *and* ONION SALAD *with* CREAMY GOAT CHEESE *and* RASPBERRY VINAIGRETTE

6 Servings ■ ▪ ■ ▪ ■ ▪ ■ ▪ ■ ▪ ■ ▪ ■ ▪ ■ ▪ ■ ▪ ■

We had friends in Colorado who kept Nubian and Swiss goats. It is the perfect terrain. The Swiss influence is found throughout the state. And so it's no surprise to find recipes that include beets, wild onion, and field greens, which grow well in the late spring, cool summers, and fall. You may use any fruity vinegar for this recipe, but I think you will agree that raspberry vinegar lends exceptional flavor to this dish. Use any combination of red and yellow beets and red and white pearl onions or wild onions when available.

RASPBERRY VINAIGRETTE

$1/4$ cup granulated sugar

$1/3$ cup raspberry vinegar

$1/2$ cup safflower oil

$1/4$ teaspoon salt

$1/4$ teaspoon black pepper

$1/4$ teaspoon fresh thyme leaves

BEET AND ONION SALAD

2 bunches fresh baby beets

1 pint pearl onions, peeled

1 tablespoon safflower oil

1 teaspoon salt

2 (5-ounce) packages goat cheese

1 (8-ounce) bag field greens to include red oak, dandelion, frisee, and arugula

Cracked black pepper to taste

Make the dressing: Combine the sugar and vinegar in a saucepan. Stir over medium-high heat until the sugar is dissolved. Cool the vinegar-sugar mixture and pour into a small mixing bowl. Whisk in the oil, salt, black pepper, and thyme. Cover with plastic wrap and keep at room temperature until ready to serve.

Oven temperature 400°F.

Make the salad: First, coat the beets and onions in a little oil, sprinkle them with salt, and scatter them in a single layer on a baking sheet; roast for 15 to 20 minutes—the beets should be al dente, firm with a bit of crunch when pierced with the tip of a sharp knife. Allow the beets and onions to cool to room temperature.

Second, transfer the cooked beets to a work surface that has been covered with waxed paper to keep the surface from staining. Use a paring knife to carefully peel the skins from the beets. Cut the beets and the larger onions in half. Leave the smaller onions whole. Transfer to a glass dish and toss with ¼ cup of the vinaigrette. Cover and refrigerate for 2 to 4 hours.

Third, cut the goat cheese while it is cold into 12 round slices. Place the slices on a sheet pan lined with parchment or plastic wrap. Allow the cheese to warm to room temperature and drizzle with a little oil.

Serve the salad: Drain the beets and onions, and toss with the field greens. Lightly dress with the vinaigrette just before serving. Arrange the salad on chilled plates and garnish with slices of the goat cheese. Finish with freshly cracked black pepper.

ROSEMARY FINGERLING POTATOES

6 Servings

Fingerling potatoes are small thumb-sized potatoes with a creamy sweet flavor. They are perfect for roasting. Rosemary and garlic lend themselves to the crusty toasted potatoes and offer a perfect complement to the trout or side dish for your favorite grilled steaks.

1 ½ **pounds fingerling potatoes**

Extra virgin olive oil

6 cloves garlic, chopped

1 **tablespoon fresh chopped rosemary**

Salt and pepper to taste

Oven temperature 400°F.

First, slice the potatoes in half lengthwise and place in a mixing bowl. Lightly coat with olive oil and toss together with the garlic and rosemary.

Second, scatter the potatoes evenly in a single layer on a baking sheet. Bake for 20 to 25 minutes. Sprinkle with salt and pepper during the final 5 minutes of baking.

SKILLET CORN *and* PEPPERS

Whether it is dripping with melted butter on the cob or added to a crunchy, savory
salad, corn is hard to beat. The sweet native grain lends a contrast of texture and flavor
to the seasoned sirloin and the delicate trout. Wrapping the cobs in foil steams the corn
in its own natural sugars and allows the butter to permeate each tender kernel.

6 ears sweet corn, shucked

1 large red bell pepper

1/2 small sweet onion

1/4 cup (1/2 stick) butter

1/4 cup chopped green onions

Salt for seasoning

First, place the ears of corn in a shallow pan with about 1/2 inch of lightly salted water. Cover tightly, bring the water to a boil over high heat, and steam the ears of corn until they are tender but still crunchy, about 4 minutes. Refresh the ears in an ice bath, and cut the kernels from the cobs with a sharp knife. Reserve the kernels and discard the cobs.

Second, cut the bell pepper in half lengthwise and remove the stem and seeds. Cut each half into three even wedges and slice each wedge into thin, julienne strips. Slice the onion into even slivers.

Third, melt the butter in a large skillet over medium-high heat. When the butter is melted and just beginning to brown, add the corn and toss for 1 minute until the corn begins to brown. Add in the onion and pepper, and reduce the heat to medium. Sauté for 2 to 3 minutes. Toss in the green onions and season with salt.

SWEET CHERRY-PLUM PANDOWDY

8 Servings

Colorado is known for its stone fruits, especially plums and cherries, which are well-suited for the cold winter temperatures and ripening summer sun. You can make this dessert with any combination of fruits, but this is my favorite! A pandowdy is a nineteenth-century classic American dessert. The dessert gets its name from the crust being "dowdied"—cut up into pieces instead of whole like a pie crust. It's sort of an upside-down pie, similar to a cobbler but made with a pie crust instead of biscuit topping.

CRUST

I 1/2 cups all-purpose flour

1/2 cup granulated sugar

2 teaspoons baking powder

I teaspoon salt

6 tablespoons (3/4 stick) unsalted butter

I large egg

6 tablespoons heavy cream

FILLING

2 cups pitted dark sweet cherries

2 cups fresh sliced black or red plums

2 teaspoons fresh lemon juice

2 tablespoons molasses

1/2 cup packed brown sugar

Pinch each of allspice, cinnamon, and ginger

1/4 cup (1/2 stick) unsalted butter

TOPPING

2 tablespoons (1/4 stick) unsalted butter, melted

1/4 cup packed brown sugar

Oven temperature 400°F.

Make the crust: First, sift the flour, sugar, baking powder, and salt into a mixing bowl. Slice the butter into 1-inch pieces and scatter over the flour mixture; then cut all of the ingredients together with a pastry cutter until the mixture resembles coarse crumbly meal.

Second, whisk the egg and cream together in a separate bowl, then add to the crumbly mixture. Stir with a wooden spoon until the dough just comes together.

Third, turn the mixture out onto a clean dry surface and knead into a pliable, tender ball. Flatten the ball by gently pressing it between your hands. Wrap the disk in plastic wrap, and chill for at least 30 minutes.

Make the filling: Combine the cherries and plums with the lemon juice and molasses in a large mixing bowl; add in the brown sugar and a

pinch each of allspice, cinnamon, and ginger. Cut the butter into tiny pieces and fold into the fruit mixture. Transfer to a well-buttered 8 x 8-inch ceramic baking dish.

Assemble the pandowdy: First, remove the chilled crust from the refrigerator and shape into a square. Roll out into a 12-inch square on a clean, lightly floured surface to a thickness of 1/4 inch, and then cut into thirty-six 2-inch squares.

Second, overlap the squares of dough to cover the filling.

Add the topping: Brush the crust with the melted butter, and sprinkle the brown sugar evenly over the top. Place the pandowdy on a sheet pan in the oven and bake until the crust is golden and the filling is bubbling through the top, 30 to 35 minutes.

Serve with either vanilla ice cream or freshly whipped cream.

Easy Time-Saving and Do-Ahead Tips

SATURDAY:

- *Clean and steam the ears of corn and cut away the kernels; prepare the onions and peppers, and refrigerate in sealed containers.*

- *Roast and peel the beets and onions.*

- *Prepare the vinaigrette.*

- *Prepare the pandowdy dough.*

SUNDAY MORNING:

- *Bake the pandowdy.*

- *Grind the pecans.*

ONE HOUR BEFORE DINNER:

- *Prepare the dredging station.*

- *Coat the trout fillets.*

Chapter 19

RISING TO MEET YOU

FRESH SWEET PEA SOUP

MUSTARD-GLAZED CORNED BEEF *with*
CABBAGE *and* BRAISED ROOT VEGETABLES

IRISH SODA BREAD

RASPBERRY-LEMON JELLY ROLL

M ay the road rise to meet you . . ."
That traditional Gaelic blessing must have haunted three Irish brothers who made their way through the squalor and din of nineteenth-century New York. Two ventured north to Boston; the other headed south and found his way to Georgia. The story of James Cross, my great-great-grandfather, is all too familiar. It's the story of the Irish in America.

Under English rule, the Irish people had essentially become serfs in their own country. The potato, most likely imported from Virginia by Sir Walter Raleigh, had turned out to be a plentiful and inexpensive food staple for these peasants. Then Ireland saw the great potato famine of the 1840s, which caused the deaths of more than a million Irish and forced another 2 million to emigrate. These are staggering statistics for a country of fewer than 8 million people.

Those who fled to America found conditions not much better than at home. Undereducated and dirt poor, they had to take the lowest-paying jobs as housemaids, factory laborers, and miners. Long workweeks, unsafe conditions, and child labor all but guaranteed a continuance of poverty. Yet these tough, lively people prevailed and made their mark. Today some 30 million Americans consider themselves of Irish descent and rich traditions of story-telling, music, and handcraftsmanship still thrive. So do the close bonds of family that have always sustained the Irish-American community.

Corned beef and cabbage have long been associated with the Irish, and in particular with their favorite holiday, St. Patrick's Day. But this wonderful dish of salt-preserved meat, also known as New England boiled dinner, was enjoyed in this country for more than a century before the mass Irish immigration began. Beef, in fact, was not common fare in Ireland, where cattle were raised almost exclusively for dairy products. The traditional Irish dish of bacon and cabbage, however, was readily changed to use corned beef, which kept well over the winter months.

As Americans began moving west—the Irish among them—they quickly grew to appreciate cured meats such as corned beef, which traveled well. During the world wars and the Great Depression, economical corned beef and cabbage became one the most popular dishes. Today this down-to-earth dish still blesses a Sunday table with a bit of an Irish lilt:

"Until we meet again, may God hold you in the hollow of His hand."

FRESH SWEET PEA SOUP

6 Servings ■ ■ ■ ■ ■ ■ ■ ■ ■ ■ ■ ■ ■ ■ ■ ■ ■ ■ ■

Using fresh peas during the spring instead of dried is a sweet take on this traditional
Irish soup. I like to brighten the sweet peas with fresh chervil and chives. You can serve
this light, satisfying soup as a simple supper, accompanied by the soda bread.

¹/₄ cup (¹/₂ stick) butter, divided

¹/₂ cup diced sweet onion

I cup thinly sliced leeks, white part only

4 cups fresh blanched peas or frozen peas, thawed

2 cups chicken broth

I tablespoon fresh chopped chervil

I tablespoon fresh snipped chives

Salt and white pepper to taste

¹/₂ cup sour cream or crème frâiche

First, melt 2 tablespoons of the butter in a saucepan over medium-low heat. When the butter begins to bubble, add in the diced onion and the sliced leeks. Sauté for 3 to 4 minutes until the onions are soft and translucent and the leeks are bright green and tender, 3 to 4 minutes.

Second, add in the remaining 2 tablespoons of butter, let it melt, and add in the peas. Cook the peas, stirring frequently, for 2 to 3 minutes. Pour in the broth, increase the heat to medium-high, and simmer until the peas are fully cooked, tender, and still bright green (6 to 8 minutes). Add in the chervil and chives. Remove the pan from heat to cool slightly.

Third, puree the mixture using a countertop or immersion blender.

To serve: Ladle the soup into wide bowls, and top each serving with a generous spoonful of sour cream or crème frâiche; then sprinkle with additional chives. Serve immediately.

MUSTARD-GLAZED CORNED BEEF *with* CABBAGE *and* BRAISED ROOT VEGETABLES

6 Servings

Corned beef gets its name from the coarse grains of salt ("corns") that were once used to cure the meat. In Vermont, corned beef is glazed with maple syrup and baked in the oven after being boiled. In other parts of New England, the glaze is made with mustard or horseradish and just a touch of honey or brown sugar. Either way, this is a truly American dish—influenced by the many immigrants who helped make our nation diverse.

CORNED BEEF

1 (3-pound) corned beef brisket

1 medium onion

1 bay leaf

2 whole cloves

2 whole cloves garlic

1 teaspoon mustard seeds

1/2 teaspoon black peppercorns

VEGETABLES

1 head green cabbage

6 medium carrots

10 to 12 small boiling onions

4 parsnips

12 to 18 small boiling potatoes

3 large turnips

1/4 cup (1/2 stick) butter

1 tablespoon fresh chopped parsley

Salt to taste

GLAZE

2 teaspoons prepared horseradish

2 tablespoons spicy brown mustard

2 tablespoons packed brown sugar

Prepare the corned beef: First, rinse the corned beef thoroughly under cold running water. Place fat side up in a large Dutch oven or braising pan, and pour in enough cold water to cover all but an inch of the meat.

Second, peel and quarter the onion, then add the onion, bay leaf, whole cloves, garlic, mustard seeds, and peppercorns into the pot with the corned beef. Bring to a boil over medium-high heat, reduce the heat to low, and skim off any residue that floats to the surface. Place the lid on the pan and simmer until the meat is fork-tender, about 2 hours.

Prepare the vegetables: First, cut the cabbage in half and then into 6 equal wedges. Cut out the core and discard. Peel the carrots and slice them into 2-inch rounds. Cut the root end from each of the boiling onions with a paring knife and peel, leaving the pointed shoot end intact to keep them from falling apart when they are cooked. Peel the parsnips and cut into 2-inch pieces. Scrub the potatoes to be cooked in their jackets. Peel the turnips and cut into quarters.

Second, when the brisket is fork-tender, remove it from the pot and place it in a shallow roasting pan, this time with the fat side down. Use a small strainer to remove the onion, bay leaf, cloves, garlic, mustard seeds, and peppercorns from the liquid. Remove and set aside about 1 cup of the cooking liquid.

Third, add the carrots, onions, parsnips, and turnips to the remaining cooking liquid in the pot. Cover with the lid, place on the stovetop and bring to a boil. Reduce the heat to medium-low and simmer for 20 minutes. Add in the potatoes and cook until the potatoes are tender, another 15 to 20 minutes.

Meanwhile, place the cabbage in a covered skillet large enough to easily hold all of the wedges. Add in enough of the reserved cooking liquid to cover the bottom of the skillet by a little more than 1/2 inch. Cover the skillet with a tight-fitting lid, set the heat to high, and steam until tender, about 15 minutes.

Prepare the glaze: Whisk together the horseradish, mustard, and brown sugar in a small bowl. While the vegetables are still cooking, use a pastry brush to coat the corned beef with the glaze. Transfer to a 325°F oven and bake until the glaze is bubbling hot, about 30 minutes. Allow the corned beef to rest in the roasting pan at room temperature until you are ready to slice, so that it stays juicy.

To serve: Place the corned beef on a clean cutting board and slice thinly against the grain with a sharp carving knife. Arrange the slices on a warm platter with the steamed cabbage, and drizzle with a little of the cooking liquid. Serve the carrots, onions, parsnips, and turnips in a separate bowl drizzled with a little more of the cooking liquid. Toss the potatoes with the butter and chopped parsley. Season them with salt and serve in a separate bowl.

IRISH SODA BREAD

2 Small Loaves

There are many variations of Irish soda bread, including tea bread with raisins and brown bread made with whole wheat flour and perhaps a little oatmeal. The basic method of preparation, however, is always the same. This variation is both hearty and rustic.

2 cups unbleached all-purpose flour

I cup cake flour

3 cups whole wheat flour

2 teaspoons baking soda

I teaspoon salt

1/4 cup (1/2 stick) unsalted butter, chilled

2 cups buttermilk

Oven temperature 450°F.

First, combine the unbleached flour, cake flour, and whole wheat flour in a large bowl and whisk well. Add the baking soda and salt, and sift together.

Second, pinch the butter into the flour mixture with the tips of your fingers until the butter is fully incorporated and "disappears" into the flour mix. Make a well in the center, pour in the buttermilk, and beat with a wooden spoon until the dough just holds together and is slightly sticky. Turn out onto a lightly floured work surface, or place in the bowl of an electric mixer fitted with a dough hook, and knead by hand or on low speed until smooth, about 6 minutes.

Third, form the dough into two 6-inch rounds and pat smooth. Dust the bottoms with a little all-purpose flour and transfer to a lightly greased baking sheet. Use a sharp thin knife to mark 6 equal wedges by scoring a 1/3-inch-deep pattern into the top of each loaf.

Fourth, place the loaves on the middle oven rack and bake for 10 minutes, then lower the temperature to 400°F and continue baking for 30 to 35 minutes. The loaves should sound hollow when tapped on the bottom. Cool completely on racks before serving.

RASPBERRY-LEMON JELLY ROLL

6 Servings

This is a wonderful, easy-to-prepare dessert made with sponge cake, raspberry jam, and lemon curd. In addition to the fresh raspberry sauce, I like to serve this dessert with fresh berries and a dollop of sweetened whipped cream.

JELLY ROLL
²/₃ cup cake flour

3 tablespoons cornstarch

¹/₄ teaspoon salt

4 large egg yolks, room temperature

Zest of 1 lemon

3/4 cup superfine sugar, divided

1 teaspoon pure vanilla extract

4 large egg whites, room temperature

Pinch of cream of tartar

Powdered sugar for dusting

¹/₂ cup seedless raspberry jam

1 (8 ounce) jar lemon curd

RASPBERRY SAUCE
2 cups fresh or frozen raspberries

¹/₂ cup granulated sugar

2 tablespoons Framboise or raspberry syrup

GLAZE
1 tablespoon fresh lemon juice

¹/₂ cup powdered sugar

Oven temperature 425°F.

Make the sponge cake: First, line a standard jelly-roll pan or 10 x 15-inch rimmed baking sheet with parchment paper that has been greased on both sides.

Second, sift the cake flour, cornstarch, and salt into a small bowl.

Third, combine the 4 egg yolks with the zest, ¹/₂ cup of the superfine sugar, and the vanilla in a separate larger bowl. Beat vigorously by hand or with a mixer on medium-high speed until the mixture is thick and pale yellow, about 3 minutes.

Fourth, place the egg whites in a stainless bowl and add a pinch of cream of tartar. Whip the mixture with clean dry beaters until it holds soft peaks. Slowly add in the remaining ¹/₄ cup superfine sugar, and continue beating until the mixture holds stiff peaks.

Fifth, stir ¹/₃ of the beaten egg white mixture into the yolk mixture, then fold the sifted flour mixture into the yolk mixture until it is fully incorporated. Fold in the remaining beaten egg whites (do this gently so the batter does not deflate). Spread the batter evenly in the prepared pan.

Sixth, bake 8 to 10 minutes until the cake is golden and springs back when gently pressed in the center. Remove the sponge cake from the oven and dust it with powdered sugar. Lay out a piece of parchment paper or a clean tea towel that has also been dusted with powdered sugar and invert the cake onto it. Carefully peel away the parchment paper that the cake was baked on, and loosely roll the cake up lengthwise (along the long edge). Allow the cake to rest at room temperature for 30 minutes.

Assemble the jelly roll: Carefully unroll the cake onto a clean dry surface. Heat the raspberry jam with a few drops of water so that it will spread easily across the entire surface of the sponge cake. Spread the jam on the cake and allow it to soak in and cool completely. Spread the lemon curd over all but the last 2 inches of the cake along the long edge of the roll. Sprinkle the jelly roll with more powdered sugar, then roll tightly in plastic wrap and refrigerate for at least 1 day and up to 3 days.

Make the raspberry sauce: In a saucepan, combine the raspberries with the sugar and Framboise or raspberry syrup. Bring the mixture to a boil over medium heat. Stirring constantly, boil the mixture for 3 minutes, until the berries are beginning to break apart and the sugar is dissolved. Reduce the heat to low and simmer for 10 to 15 minutes. Remove from the heat and pass through a fine sieve, pressing all the pulp firmly through the sieve with a rubber spatula. Discard the seeds that remain in the sieve, and let the sauce cool.

Make the lemon glaze: Take the jelly roll out of the refrigerator and unwrap. In a small bowl, blend the lemon juice into the powdered sugar. Use a pastry brush to glaze the top and sides of the roll with the syrup. Keep the jelly roll uncovered and at room temperature until ready to serve.

To serve: Trim away each end of the roll with a thin serrated knife, then cut the jelly roll into 6 even slices. Arrange the slices on plates and pour a little raspberry sauce over each. Dust with powdered sugar, and serve immediately.

Easy Time-Saving and Do-Ahead Tips

SATURDAY:

- Prepare the soup to be reheated on Sunday.
- Bake and completely assemble the jelly roll.
- Sift dry ingredients for the soda bread.

SUNDAY MORNING:

- Prepare the vegetables and refrigerate in well-sealed containers.
- Cook the corned beef, and prepare the mustard glaze.

AN HOUR AND A HALF BEFORE DINNER:

- Bake the soda bread.
- Glaze the jelly roll.

Chapter 20

AN ANCIENT HERITAGE

SALAD *of* SPINACH, CUCUMBER, *and*
RADISH *with* LEMON YOGURT DRESSING

SUCCULENT HERB-SCENTED LEG *of* SPRING
LAMB *with* ROASTED RED-SKINNED POTATOES

GRILLED ZUCCHINI *with* EGGPLANT,
FETA, *and* TOMATOES

RUSTIC VILLAGE BREAD

ORANGE-SOAKED HONEY-WALNUT CAKE

Americans come from diverse backgrounds. Our families are themselves a melting pot. As a nation of immigrants, ours is a diverse tapestry. From among the nations of the world, we gather on one common ground. Learning about the history of our ancestral inheritance, with the varying customs and observances, adds untold and unmeasured riches to our lives.

The Sunday meal is a terrific means to explore our heritage by exploring the foods of our immigrant parents, grandparents, or great grandparents—the time-honored regional American foods enjoyed from generation to generation. Preparing that special heirloom dish brings us in touch with our roots and the old-world celebrations. Tradition is the thread that ties us to history—our history and our heritage.

Just as every recipe tells a story, so too, do the heirloom treasures we bring out to grace our tables. When we set our table with that special vase, bowl, or hand-crafted cloth, we touch the past. To learn about our ancestors is to learn about ourselves. To learn of their struggles and their faith is to find strength in our past and the inspiration to carry on. To continue the legacy is to weave our own threads of experience into a tapestry woven long ago.

The Greek influence on America is considerable. From the U.S. Capitol and Supreme Court to our public libraries and the neo-classical columns of the White House, Greek architecture points to our shared ideals of democracy, self-governance, and the Arts.

Then on Easter Sunday your fasting would be over and the celebration would begin with roast lamb, dripping and juicy, seasoned and paired with potatoes or baked orzo, and deliciously supplemented with briny olives, stuffed grape leaves, fresh and roasted vegetables, a bounty of cheeses, and rustic breads. But first, everyone around the table would take a bright dyed-red egg and crack it against that held by one's neighbor, celebrating the sound echoing that of the stone rolled away from the tomb. As you broke the eggs, you also would exchange a traditional blessing, emphasizing the joy of the Easter feast:

"Christos Anesti"—Christ is risen!

"Alithos Anesti"—Indeed, He is risen!

SALAD *of* SPINACH, CUCUMBER, *and* RADISH *with* LEMON YOGURT DRESSING

8 Servings ▪▪▪▪▪▪▪▪▪▪▪▪▪▪▪▪▪▪▪▪▪▪▪▪▪▪▪▪▪

Crisp salads made with fresh vegetables are served in nearly every country. Generally they are simply dressed, like this one—with olive oil, lemon, and herbs. Serve this salad with thick slices of rustic village bread accompanied by tiny bowls of extra-virgin olive oil for dipping the bread in and a variety of cured olives for all to enjoy.

SALAD

2 (8-ounce) bags baby spinach leaves

1 cucumber, peeled and thinly sliced

8 radishes, trimmed and thinly sliced

1 bunch green onions, thinly sliced

DRESSING

2 whole cloves garlic, peeled

1/2 teaspoon coarse salt

1 teaspoon granulated sugar

2 tablespoons fresh lemon juice

1 cup plain yogurt

1/4 cup extra virgin olive oil

1/4 teaspoon coarse-ground black pepper

1 tablespoon fresh chopped dill

1 tablespoon fresh chopped parsley

Make the salad: Thoroughly rinse the spinach leaves in cold water to refresh them and discard any tough stems or wilted leaves. Shake the spinach dry in a colander covered with a clean tea towel or in a salad spinner. Toss the spinach with the sliced cucumber, radishes, and green onions. Refrigerate in a salad bowl covered with a damp paper towel or plastic wrap until you are ready to serve.

Prepare the dressing: Combine the garlic cloves in a small mixing bowl with the salt and sugar; use a fork to mash them into a paste. Whisk in the lemon juice and the yogurt, and slowly whisk in the extra virgin olive oil until blended. Season to taste with the pepper.

Serve the salad: Just before serving, add the freshly chopped dill and parsley to the refrigerated salad and lightly toss together with the dressing.

SUCCULENT HERB-SCENTED LEG *of* SPRING LAMB *with* ROASTED RED-SKINNED POTATOES

8 Servings

There was a time when many Americans ignored lamb. We were, after all, a wide-open country known for raising and eating beef. That has changed somewhat in the past decade or two, and once you've tasted this seasoned lamb, you'll understand why. Lamb is a traditional Easter dish throughout much of the world. Certainly it is perfect in spring, but lamb is wonderful any time of the year.

Have your butcher bone out the leg of lamb, keeping the shank attached and trimming away any excess fat, and then butterfly it for easy preparation.

LAMB

1 (6-pound) leg of lamb, semi-boned and butterflied

6 whole cloves garlic, minced

2 tablespoons fresh chopped rosemary, divided

1/2 cup packed fresh basil leaves

1/4 cup packed fresh mint leaves

2 tablespoons cracked peppercorns

2 lemons, halved, seeds removed

1/4 cup olive oil

Coarse salt to season

POTATOES

2 pounds small red-skinned potatoes

2 tablespoons olive oil

1 tablespoon fresh chopped rosemary

2 cloves garlic, thinly sliced

Salt and pepper to taste

Oven temperature 450°F.

Make the lamb: First, place the lamb cut side up on a clean work surface. Sprinkle the garlic evenly over the inside of the lamb and sprinkle with half of the chopped rosemary. Lay the basil and mint leaves over the rosemary, then roll the lamb leg back into its natural shape.

Second, tie the lamb securely with kitchen twine, knotting it every 2 inches. Rub the remaining rosemary and the cracked peppercorns into the exterior surface of the lamb. Squeeze the halved lemons over the lamb and drizzle with the olive oil. Cover with plastic wrap and refrigerate overnight or for up to 24 hours.

Third, remove the lamb from the refrigerator. Sprinkle it with coarse salt and allow it to rest for 30 minutes at room temperature.

Fourth, place the lamb in a shallow roasting pan. Adjust the lower rack near the bottom of the oven. Roast the lamb for 15 minutes, then reduce the heat to 325°F and cook for 1 hour longer—the roast should be rare at this point.

To make the potatoes: Cut each potato in half and toss them with the olive oil, rosemary, and garlic. Season with salt and pepper. After the lamb has roasted for 1 hour and 15 minutes, scatter the potatoes around the roasting pan and continue baking until a meat thermometer inserted into the thickest part of the lamb reaches 140°F, about 20 to 25 min. Remove the lamb from the pan and place it on a clean cutting board.

Meanwhile, increase the oven temperature to 400°F and spread the potatoes evenly around the roasting pan. Return the potatoes to the oven and let them continue baking until they are fully cooked and browned, about 15 minutes.

Serve the lamb and potatoes: Carefully cut away the kitchen twine. Hold the lamb at the shank end and evenly slice the meat with a sharp carving knife. Transfer the lamb to a warm platter. Scatter the potatoes around the meat. Pour the juices from the pan and the cutting board over the meat.

GRILLED ZUCCHINI *with* EGGPLANT, FETA, *and* TOMATOES

8 Servings ■

The Mediterranean flavors in this easy-to-prepare dish showcase the sweetness of the grilled vegetables, the garlicky topping, and the sharp feta cheese. This is a wonderfully sensuous dish.

VEGETABLES

2 medium eggplants, peeled and cut lengthwise into ¹/₂-inch-thick slices

Coarse salt

4 medium zucchini, cut lengthwise into ¹/₃-inch slices

2 medium onions, peeled and sliced ¹/₃-inch thick

¹/₄ cup olive oil

TOPPING

2 tablespoons extra virgin olive oil

2 cloves garlic, minced

2 tablespoons diced onion

4 cups peeled, seeded, and diced tomatoes

2 teaspoons fresh chopped mint leaves

Salt and pepper to taste

2 cups crumbled feta cheese, divided

Sprinkle the eggplant slices with coarse salt and place in a colander for 30 minutes to drain the bitter juices. Rinse and pat dry with paper towels. Brush the slices of zucchini, onion, and eggplant with olive oil and season with a little salt.

Grill the vegetables directly over high heat, turning them once: 6 to 8 minutes for the eggplant, 4 to 5 minutes for the onion, and 2 to 3 minutes for the zucchini.

Prepare the topping: Heat the extra virgin olive oil in a skillet over medium heat. Sauté the garlic and onion until translucent, 2 to 3 minutes. Toss in the tomatoes and simmer until the liquid is reduced, 4 to 5 minutes. Add in the chopped mint leaves, season to taste with salt and pepper, remove from the heat, and set aside.

Oven temperature 325°F.

Assemble the casserole: Arrange the grilled slices of eggplant on the bottom of a lightly oiled 13 x 9-inch casserole, followed by the onion, and then the zucchini. Cover with 1^1/$_3$ cups of the crumbled feta cheese and the tomato topping. Bake for 20 to 25 minutes. Increase the temperature to 400°F, sprinkle the top of the casserole with the remaining ^{2}/$_3$ cup feta and bake for an additional 10 to 15 minutes.

RUSTIC VILLAGE BREAD

1 Round Loaf

Making great bread is a simple act of love; it takes time, patience, and nurturing. This rustic loaf is even more reminiscent of village life when it is baked on a pizza stone. As with all breads that are made with whole-grain flour, additional rising time is required—but the reward is well worth the wait.

1 package (1 1/2 teaspoons) active dry yeast

1/4 cup warm water, about 110°F

1 tablespoon honey

1 tablespoon olive oil

1/4 cup plain yogurt

1 cup water, room temperature

1 cup whole wheat flour

1 1/2 cups bread flour, divided

1/2 cup wheat germ

1 1/2 teaspoons coarse salt

Oven temperature 400°F.

Make the bread: First, sprinkle the yeast over the warm water and let stand for 1 minute. Then stir with a wooden spoon until the yeast is dissolved.

Second, whisk the honey, olive oil, and yogurt together in a mixing bowl until blended. Whisk in the room temperature water and the dissolved yeast. Use a wooden spoon to stir in the whole wheat flour and 1/2 cup of the bread flour. Continue stirring until the mixture is smooth and elastic, about 200 strokes. The dough will now have the consistency of a thick batter. Scrape down the sides of the bowl with a rubber spatula. Cover with a clean tea towel and set in a draft-free place until the dough is bubbly and has doubled in volume, about 1 1/2 hours.

Third, whisk the remaining bread flour together with the wheat germ and salt in a separate bowl. Use an electric mixer fitted with a dough hook to slowly incorporate the flour mixture into the bubbly dough, adding in extra flour as needed a tablespoon at a time, until the dough pulls away from the bowl and forms a ball. Knead on low speed for about 8 minutes—the dough should be densely textured and stiff enough to hold its shape.

Fourth, lightly coat the dough with a little olive oil, place it into a clean bowl and cover with a clean tea towel. Allow it to rise in a warm, draft-free place until it has doubled in volume, about 1 hour.

Fifth, place the dough on a lightly floured work surface and knead for about 1 minute. Shape into a smooth ball. Flatten the ball into a 7-inch-round loaf and score a 1/4-inch-deep cross-cut on the top, using a sharp knife. Brush with a little water. Cover the loaf with a clean tea towel and let it rise for 45 minutes.

Sixth, brush the loaf lightly with olive oil and sprinkle with a pinch of coarse salt. Transfer the loaf to a pizza stone or a baking sheet dusted with cornmeal and bake for 30 to 35 minutes. When it is done, the bread will have a dark-brown crust and sound hollow when tapped on the bottom.

ORANGE-SOAKED HONEY-WALNUT CAKE

12 Servings ▮▬▬▮▬▬▮▬▬▮▬▬▮▬▬▮▬▬▮▬▬▮▬▬▮▬

This moist, delicious, traditional cake is made without butter or milk, making it a perfect choice for Lent. It is an example of the various recipes found throughout the ancient world that have been added to the ever-changing American table, where they are savored and served as a "taste of home" on holidays and at family gatherings. Sunday dinner is one such time.

CAKE

2 1/2 cups all-purpose flour

1/2 cup fresh white breadcrumbs

2 teaspoons baking powder

1 teaspoon baking soda

1/2 teaspoon cinnamon

1/4 teaspoon salt

4 egg whites, room temperature

Pinch cream of tartar

1 cup vegetable oil

1 1/2 cups granulated sugar

1/4 cup honey

4 large egg yolks, room temperature

1 cup freshly squeezed orange juice

1 cup finely ground walnuts

ORANGE SYRUP

3/4 cup granulated sugar

1/2 cup water

1 cinnamon stick

2 tablespoons honey

3/4 cup freshly squeezed orange juice

Zest of 1 orange

Oven temperature 350°F.

Make the cake: First, combine the flour and fresh breadcrumbs with the baking powder, baking soda, cinnamon, and salt in a mixing bowl and whisk together thoroughly.

Second, combine the egg whites with the cream of tartar in a separate bowl. Beat the whites using an electric mixer and clean dry beaters until they hold their peaks and are stiff but not dry.

Third, combine the vegetable oil, sugar, and honey in the bowl of an electric mixer fitted with a balloon whisk. Blend on medium speed until the sugar and honey are dissolved; then blend in the egg yolks. Fit the electric mixer with a paddle attachment and slowly add the dry ingredients in 3 batches alternately with the orange juice, mixing just enough after each addition for all the ingredients to fully blend together. Use a rubber spatula to gently fold in the beaten egg whites, followed by the ground walnuts.

Fourth, spoon the batter into a lightly greased and floured 10-inch Bundt pan. Place the pan on the middle oven rack and bake about 50 minutes until a wooden pick comes out clean when inserted into the center of the cake. When the cake is done, remove it from the oven and place on a cooling rack for 10 minutes. Turn the cake out onto a rack and let it cool for 20 to 30 minutes while you prepare the orange syrup.

Prepare the orange syrup: Mix the sugar into the water and bring to a boil, stirring constantly to dissolve all the sugar. Add in the cinnamon stick, honey, orange juice, and orange zest. Turn the heat down to medium and simmer until the liquid reduces to 1 cup of syrup, about 20 minutes. Discard the cinnamon stick.

Glaze the cake: Brush the warm syrup over the outside of the warm cake, allowing it to soak in. Continue to brush on the glaze until all of the syrup is absorbed.

Easy Time-Saving and Do-Ahead Tips

SATURDAY:

- Bake the honey-walnut cake and soak with the orange syrup.
- Marinate the lamb.
- Bake the bread.
- Prepare the salad dressing and refrigerate.

SUNDAY MORNING:

- Prepare the salad vegetables and refrigerate.
- Peel and slice the vegetables for the eggplant casserole; refrigerate in well-sealed containers.

TWO AND A HALF HOURS BEFORE DINNER:

- Remove the roast from the refrigerator and bring to room temperature.
- Grill casserole vegetables and assemble the casserole.

Chapter 21

SUNDAY *in the* NORTHWEST

GOLDEN MUSHROOM *and* ONION SOUP

BAKED PACIFIC HALIBUT *with*
LEMON-CAPER BUTTER

BUTTERED NEW POTATOES *and* DILL
STEAMED ASPARAGUS SPEARS

STRAWBERRY POPPY SEED SHORTCAKES

My grandmother always called the Pacific Northwest "God's country," and I can understand why. From the vast wilderness of Alaska down through the settled greenery of Oregon, this region offers untold bounty in a world of wonder. There are dramatic snow-capped mountain peaks, cascading whitewater streams, giant red cedars piercing forest canopies, and churning ocean waves crashing on the rugged coast. The contrast to the dusty red flatlands of her native west Texas must have taken my grandmother's breath away.

It takes my breath away, too. I've lived and traveled extensively through this beautiful region. I've hiked in the Cascades and camped deep within the rainforest of the Olympic Peninsula. I've climbed great driftwood piles along rocky beaches and watched the sunset off Oregon's spectacular Coos Bay. I've followed the headwaters of the Spokane River from Idaho into Washington, crossed the mighty Columbia, and traversed the pastoral Willamette Valley. Each memory transports me to a place that is like no other.

When it comes to food, each state in this bountiful region boasts something special. Washington is known for great apples and sweet onions; Alaska for deepwater crab and halibut; Oregon for fine fruits and cheeses, especially Anjou pears and the excellent Tillamook cheddar. Berries abound everywhere in the cool climate. Untamed rivers teem with salmon, steelhead, and rainbow trout. Wild asparagus sprout along a river's edge. And earthy mushrooms shoot up through fern-covered forest floors.

At one time this was all Russian territory, stretching south from the Bering Sea to California's Monterey coast (the first Russian Orthodox mission was established on Kodiak Island in 1794). Fur trapping was the main endeavor. Five years after Lewis and Clark ended their cross-country expedition near the mouth of the Columbia in 1805, Vincent Astor established the Pacific Fur Company. The Scandinavian population grew—today, Astoria still boasts a large population of Americans with Finish ancestry. When my grandparents came to the Northwest with the railroad one hundred years later, the main industries were still fishing, trapping, and timber. Cities like Seattle and Portland were little more than oversized villages. They found a welcoming place.

You'll find a welcome place, too. You'll also find a bounty of fresh ingredients made for a Sunday celebration. Here is a menu that reflects both the natural abundance of the region and its unique history with unpretentious, delicately seasoned foods that boast rich yet natural unadorned flavors.

GOLDEN MUSHROOM
and ONION SOUP

▪ ▬ ▬ ▬ ▪ ▬ ▬ ▬ ▪ ▬ ▬ ▬ ▪ ▬ ▬ ▬ ▪ ▬ ▬ ▬ ▪ ▬ ▬ ▬ ▪ ▬ ▬ ▬ ▪

Wild mushrooms are abundant throughout the Northwest, especially in the spring and early fall, and their aroma and earthy flavors are intense and heady. The variety of wild forest mushrooms being foraged and brought to market has dramatically increased over the past several years. I like to combine fresh button, cremini, and shiitakes with wood ear and chanterelles (do not use portabellas—their dark juices will make for an unappealing soup). I prefer to use sweet Walla Walla or Vidalia onions.

1 pound assorted fresh mushrooms

1 rib celery with leaves, chopped

1 leek, white part only, chopped

1 sprig fresh thyme

6 cups chicken broth

2 medium sweet onions

1/2 cup (1 stick) butter, divided

4 cloves garlic, thinly sliced

Pinch of salt

1/2 cup fruity white wine or white grape juice

2 chicken bouillon cubes or 2 tablespoons concentrated chicken stock

1 1/2 tablespoons cornstarch

1 1/2 cups half-and-half

Salt to taste

1 tablespoon fresh snipped chives

First, clean the mushrooms with a damp paper towel and remove the stems. Combine the mushroom stems, celery, leek, and thyme with the chicken broth in a 4-quart saucepan and bring to a boil over medium heat. Let the broth boil for 2 to 3 minutes, then remove from heat, cover with a tight-fitting lid and steep for about 25 minutes to infuse the broth with the mushroom flavor. Strain the seasoned broth through a fine sieve into a bowl, and discard the stems and vegetables.

Second, cut the onions in half crosswise and then slice the halves into slivers. Slice the mushrooms into varying thicknesses. Heat 1/4 cup of the butter in a heavy-bottomed skillet over high heat until it just begins to brown. Sprinkle the slivered onions in the butter, reduce the heat to medium-high, add in the garlic, and caramelize until the onions are amber in color, 6 to 8 minutes.

Third, make a well in the middle of the cara-melized onions by pushing them to the edges of the skillet. Melt the remaining 1/4 cup of butter in the well, add in the sliced mushrooms, and toss lightly with the butter. Sauté for 3 to 4 min-utes without stirring, then toss the mushrooms together with the onions, and season with a pinch of salt.

Fourth, add the wine or grape juice to the skil-let and scrape the bottom to loosen any browned bits, then pour in the reserved mushroom broth. Simmer until the mushrooms are tender but still meaty and firm-fleshed, about 5 minutes. Strain the soup through a fine sieve into a bowl. Reserve the mushrooms and onions. Return the strained liquid to the skillet and place over medium heat. When it begins to simmer, add the chicken bouil-lon cubes.

Fifth, thoroughly whisk the cornstarch with the half-and-half in a small bowl, and pour it into the broth. Simmer for 4 to 5 minutes, stirring occa-sionally. Add in the reserved mushrooms and onions and simmer for a few minutes more. Sea-son to taste with salt, fold in the snipped chives, and serve immediately.

BAKED PACIFIC HALIBUT *with* LEMON-CAPER BUTTER

6 Servings ■■■■■■■■■■■■■■■■■■■■■■■■■■■■

Pacific halibut swim in the cold waters from the Bering Straits to the Santa Barbara Islands. Their delicate flavor, firm texture, and snow-white color make halibut a highly prized catch.

LEMON-CAPER BUTTER

1/2 **cup (I stick) unsalted butter**

I **tablespoon minced capers**

2 **tablespoons minced green onion**

2 **tablespoons fresh lemon juice**

HALIBUT

6 **(6-ounce) halibut fillets**

I **teaspoon coarse salt**

3 **tablespoons Dijon mustard**

I 1/2 **cups fresh white breadcrumbs**

I **tablespoon chopped parsley**

2 **lemons, halved**

Oven temperature 400°F.

Prepare the lemon-caper butter: Combine the butter, capers, green onion, and lemon juice in the bowl of a food processor fitted with a steel blade. Pulse to blend and set aside.

Prepare the halibut: First, lightly salt each fillet. Smear the Dijon mustard over the top and sides of each fillet and coat with the breadcrumbs and parsley.

Second, coat the bottom of a baking sheet with half of the lemon-caper butter. Place the fillets skin side down on the buttered pan, and dot each fillet with the remaining butter. Bake until the fish is crusty and golden on the outside and moist and flaky in the middle, 15 to 18 minutes.

Third, transfer the baked fish to a warm platter. Squeeze the lemons into the butter and drippings that remain on the baking sheet. Whisk together thoroughly and pour over the fish.

BUTTERED NEW POTATOES *and* DILL STEAMED ASPARAGUS SPEARS

6 Servings

We often take foods for granted by dressing them up and effectively masking their subtle and wonderful flavor. Buttered new potatoes and tender asparagus seem like they were made to accompany a delicate fish like halibut—why else would we serve them together so often? Simple is sometimes best.

POTATOES

18 to 24 small new potatoes, peeled

1/2 cup (1 stick) butter

Salt and white pepper to taste

Make the potatoes: First, place the potatoes in a large pot. Cover with water and season with a little salt. Bring the water to a boil over high heat, reduce the heat to medium, and simmer until you can just pierce the potatoes with the tip of a knife, 12 to 15 minutes.

Second, drain and season the potatoes with salt and white pepper, then add the butter into the pot. Cover and let the butter melt for 4 to 5 minutes. Toss the potatoes with the melted butter just before serving.

ASPARAGUS

1 1/2 pounds fresh asparagus spears, trimmed

2 tablespoons butter

1 leek, white part only, thinly sliced

1 tablespoon fresh chopped dill

Pinch of salt

Prepare the asparagus: First, blanch the asparagus by dropping them into a shallow pan filled with boiling salted water. Cook for 3 to 4 minutes, then immediately plunge into a bowl of ice water to stop the cooking process. Remove the spears after 2 minutes and drain and dry thoroughly.

Second, spread the butter over the bottom of a skillet and sprinkle the leeks evenly onto the butter. Lay the blanched asparagus over the leeks and season with the chopped dill and a pinch of salt. Cover with a tight-fitting lid and steam just enough to heat the asparagus through, 2 to 3 minutes.

STRAWBERRY POPPY SEED SHORTCAKES

6 Servings

I often made shortcakes at Blair House for special guests that I knew would enjoy a true all-American treat. These are very special: They are tender and buttery—sublime when served with the fresh strawberry sauce and mounds of sweetened cream.

SHORTCAKES
1 1/2 tablespoons pure vanilla extract

1 tablespoon poppy seeds

1 cup all-purpose flour

1 cup cake flour

2 teaspoons baking powder

3/4 teaspoon baking soda

1/4 teaspoon salt

1/2 cup plus 2 tablespoons (1 1/4 sticks) unsalted butter

6 tablespoons superfine sugar

1 large egg, room temperature

1/3 cup heavy cream

STRAWBERRY SAUCE
1 dry pint strawberries

1/4 cup granulated sugar

SHORTCAKE FILLING
1 dry pint strawberries

Granulated sugar to taste

1 1/2 cups heavy whipping cream

6 tablespoons granulated sugar

Powdered sugar for dusting

Make the shortcakes: First, warm the vanilla extract over low heat in a small stainless pan or in a glass dish in the microwave. Add the poppy seeds to the warm vanilla, and soak them for 2 hours. This will soften the poppy seeds and allow them to absorb the vanilla flavor.

Oven temperature 450°F.

Second, sift the all-purpose flour, cake flour, baking powder, baking soda, and salt into a mixing bowl.

Third, slice the butter into 1-inch pieces and scatter the pieces over the top of the flour mixture. Sprinkle the superfine sugar and vanilla-soaked poppy seeds over the top. Cut all the ingredients together with a pastry cutter until the mixture resembles coarse crumbly meal.

Fourth, combine the egg and cream in a separate bowl and whisk until frothy, about 1 minute. Add to the crumbly mixture and stir until the dough holds together and attains the consistency of moist, slightly sticky biscuit dough. Knead gently until smooth, about 1 minute.

Fifth, dust the dough with a little flour and form into a log that is about 6 inches long and $2^{1}/_{2}$ inches in diameter. Place the log on a clean, lightly floured work surface and cut into 6 even slices. Gently reshape the slices into flat rounds and pat smooth. Brush the tops with a little heavy cream and sprinkle with a little granulated sugar.

Sixth, transfer the shortcakes to an ungreased baking sheet and bake for 12 to 15 minutes. They will spread and rise until double in size with golden cracked tops. Cool completely on the baking sheet before serving.

Make the strawberry sauce: First, wash and then hull the strawberries. Slice into halves and place in a saucepan. Add the sugar and bring to a simmer over medium heat, stirring continuously until the sugar is dissolved, about 3 minutes.

Second, simmer undisturbed until the berries begin to fall apart, about 20 minutes. Then remove from the heat and strain through a sieve into a small stainless bowl. Use a wooden spoon to press on the berries, scraping hard to extract all of the pulp. Scrape the pulp from the outside of the sieve and add to the sauce, then cover and refrigerate. Discard the solids left in the sieve.

Prepare the filling: First, wash and hull the strawberries, then slice into a stainless mixing bowl and sweeten to taste with sugar. Allow the berries to rest at room temperature for 20 minutes so that the berries absorb the sweetness of the sugar and the juices combine to form a syrup.

Second, pour the cream into the chilled bowl of a mixer and add the sugar. Mix with a chilled balloon whisk at medium speed until the sugar has dissolved, 3 to 4 minutes. Then whip on high until stiff peaks hold, about 2 more minutes. Cover and refrigerate until ready to use.

Assemble the shortcakes: Use a thin serrated knife to split each cake in half horizontally. Place the bottom layers on dessert plates, and spoon a little strawberry sauce over each, letting it run onto the plate. Follow with a dollop of whipped cream. Divide the strawberry filling between the shortcakes, and drizzle a little of their natural syrup over each. Mound with more whipped cream, and then replace the biscuit tops. Drizzle the remaining strawberry sauce around the assembled shortcakes, and dust the tops with powdered sugar. If desired, garnish with rosettes of the whipped cream and a whole fresh strawberry. Serve immediately.

Easy Time-Saving and Do-Ahead Tips

SATURDAY:

- Prepare the soup and refrigerate.
- Cut the halibut into serving portions.
- Blanch the asparagus and prepare the leeks.
- Prepare the strawberry sauce.
- Prepare the lemon-caper butter for the halibut.

SUNDAY MORNING:

- Bake the poppy seed shortcakes.

ONE HOUR BEFORE DINNER:

- Season and coat the halibut fillets.
- Peel the potatoes.
- Clean and slice the strawberries.
- Whip the cream and refrigerate.

Chapter 22

ALONG THE KING'S HIGHWAY

ALMOND RICE PILAF

CHILLED GAZPACHO

BRAISED GAME HENS *with* LEMON,
OREGANO, *and* GREEN OLIVES

MINTED CANTALOUPE SORBET

It's called the King's Highway, but it's really the mission road. California's El Camino Real connects past and present just as it connects one centuries-old Franciscan mission to another. Twenty-one of these self-sufficient outposts once marked this beautiful byway, each a long day's journey from the other across rugged California ranch country, each an oasis for the weary traveler. Most of the missions still stand today. The King's Highway winds its way between them from San Diego to Sonoma County, its 600 miles marked by bells cast in concrete and cast iron. They are mute reminders of the mission bells that once echoed across the sunny landscape.

California was first explored by the Spanish and was later part of the vast Mexican empire. In the late 1700s while our English-speaking founding fathers fought to establish their own country, Spanish-speaking Franciscan monks in California, led by Father Juniper Sierra, were laboring to establish a different kind of society. The agrarian society envisioned by Father Sierra proved far-reaching. California's fertile and fruitful agricultural enterprise owes much to those early efforts. Franciscans introduced oranges, avocados, melons, tomatoes, olives, (mission) figs, grapes, wine, and brandy into the Golden State.

The Mediterranean influences found throughout California are not limited to the Spanish. The central Californian coast boasts one of the largest Portuguese-American populations in the country, whose ancestors found along the central coast a climate and terrain more than similar to the western Iberian Peninsula and helped found the fishing, canning, and dairy industries. During the Gold Rush, Italian immigrants came in droves and found gold as well in farming, fishing, and wine making.

The culinary influences in our lives are many. The Mediterranean and New World flavors are among those I savor. Along El Camino Real we find an array of fresh flavors and vibrant colors that are perfect for today's lighter style of cooking.

I often think back to the California of my childhood and to the dreams of Juniper Sierra: We all seek refuge from an encroaching world, a place of rest along the highway of life. Like the tranquil missions along El Camino Real, Sunday offers us a respite, an opportunity to lay down our burdens and truly relax. So take a drive along the King's Highway. Spend time beneath the bay laurel trees, caressed by the gentle breeze. And be sure to stop in the sleepy midday quiet to listen once more for the sound of mission bells.

ALMOND RICE PILAF

Pilaf is traditionally baked in an oven after the grains are browned, rather than being steamed— it gives the rice a nutty texture and flavor, one that goes well with the almonds. California is one the country's largest rice producers and the premiere almond producer—a natural fit.

3 tablespoons olive oil

1/2 cup diced onion

1/2 cup rough chopped almonds

1 1/2 cups long-grain or basmati rice

3 cups chicken broth

1 bay leaf

Oven temperature 325°F.

Heat the olive oil in a heavy-bottomed, oven-proof pan over medium heat. Add in the onion and sauté for 2 minutes, until the onions are soft. Add the almonds and continue to cook 1 minute more. Increase the heat to medium high, add in the rice, and sauté the mixture, stirring often, until the rice and almonds are beginning to brown and the onions have begun to caramelize, 3 to 4 minutes. Pour in the chicken broth and stir until it begins to simmer. Add the bay leaf, cover tightly, and cook for 20 minutes. Allow the rice to stand undisturbed for 5 minutes. Remove the bay leaf, and toss the rice with a fork.

CHILLED GAZPACHO

6 Servings

Gazpacho is a cold soup that is often thought to have originated in Spain, but the traditional ingredients—tomatoes and peppers—found their way to Spain from Mexico during the age of exploration. There are countless ways to prepare this classic summer soup. I like to caramelize the garlic and onions to bring out their sweetness and use tomato paste as the binder instead of bread. The seasoned shrimp add body and provide a wonderful vibrant contrast of flavor, texture, and color.

SHRIMP

1/4 cup extra virgin olive oil, divided

2 cloves garlic, minced

1 teaspoon crushed red pepper

1 tablespoon fresh chopped basil

18 medium shrimp (about 1 pound), peeled and deveined, with tails

Pinch of salt

1 lemon, halved

GAZPACHO

1/4 cup extra virgin olive oil

4 whole cloves garlic

1 medium onion, diced

6 ripe tomatoes, peeled, seeded, and diced

1/2 teaspoon chili powder

Pinch of salt

Pinch of pepper

2 cups tomato or V-8 juice

1 tablespoon tomato paste

1 tablespoon fresh chopped basil

1 teaspoon red wine vinegar

1 teaspoon Worcestershire sauce

1/2 teaspoon Tabasco sauce

1 1/2 cups peeled, seeded, and diced cucumber

3/4 cup diced green bell pepper

3/4 cup diced yellow bell pepper

1/2 cup chopped green onions

Salt and pepper to taste

Marinate the shrimp: First, mix together 2 tablespoons of the extra virgin olive oil, garlic, crushed red pepper, and basil in a stainless mixing bowl. Toss the shrimp, coating thoroughly, and spread evenly in a ceramic dish. Cover and marinate in the refrigerator for at least 4 hours and up to 24 hours.

Cook the shrimp: Pour the remaining olive oil into a skillet over medium-high heat and quickly add the shrimp. Sauté undisturbed for 2 to 3 minutes. Season with a pinch of salt, and turn each of the shrimp using a pair of kitchen tongs. Squeeze the lemon over the shrimp and continue cooking until they are firm, pink, and just cooked, about 1 minute. Transfer to a ceramic dish and cool to room temperature.

Make the gazpacho: First, heat the extra virgin olive oil in a heavy skillet over medium-high heat. Sauté the whole garlic cloves, turning every so often until they just begin to brown, 3 to 4 minutes. Add in the onion and continue cooking to caramelize, 4 to 5 minutes. Stir in the diced tomatoes and sauté for 2 minutes. Add in the chili powder, a pinch of salt and pepper, and the tomato juice. Simmer for 1 minute. Whisk in the tomato paste, simmer for 1 minute, and remove the skillet from the heat. Add the chopped basil, the vinegar, Worcestershire, and Tabasco. Cool to room temperature.

Second, pour the cooled mixture into the bowl of a food processor fitted with a steel blade. Pulse just enough to blend (it should be chunky).

Third, combine the diced cucumber, bell peppers, and green onions in a mixing bowl. Mix all but 6 tablespoons of the combined vegetables into the soup and adjust the seasoning to taste. Cover and refrigerate for at least 4 hours and up to 24 hours.

Serve the soup: Ladle the soup into chilled bowls. Mound 1 tablespoon of the reserved vegetables into the center of each bowl of soup, and set 3 of the cooked shrimp around the little mound of vegetables. Garnish, if desired, with fresh basil leaves and lime juice.

BRAISED GAME HENS *with* LEMON, OREGANO, *and* GREEN OLIVES

6 Servings ■ ■ ■ ■ ■ ■ ■ ■ ■ ■ ■ ■ ■ ■ ■ ■ ■ ■

This simple, peasant-style dish captures and celebrates a by-gone era with its harmony of natural flavors. This is a childhood favorite of mine that my mom used to make and serve with a festive salad. My mother was a remarkable cook, and we grew up eating a variety of food. Game hens were often served on Sundays. This dish can be prepared using Mexican oregano, which is stronger than the more common varieties. But I prefer the sweeter Italian or Turkish oregano, which is a member of the mint family and has hints of rosemary and marjoram.

MARINADE

1/3 cup olive oil

2 cloves garlic, minced

2 tablespoons fresh chopped oregano

1/2 teaspoon crushed red pepper

2 teaspoons ground cumin seeds

2 teaspoons grated lemon zest

3 medium lemons

GAME HENS

6 game hens, 18- to 20-ounces each

Coarse salt for seasoning

1 cup olive oil

2 heads garlic, broken into cloves

1/2 cup dry white wine

1 (10-ounce) jar cracked green olives, drained

Lemon peel

6 sprigs fresh oregano

1 medium lemon

3/4 cup chicken broth

Marinate the game hens: First, combine the olive oil with the garlic, oregano, crushed red pepper, cumin, and lemon zest in a small mixing bowl. Use a vegetable peeler to peel the rind from the remaining lemons. Seal the lemon peel and the peeled lemons in plastic to keep them from drying out.

Second, evenly spread the marinade all over the outside and inside of each hen. Insert half a peeled lemon inside each game hen, and then tie their legs together and secure the wings with kitchen twine. Place the hens in a ceramic dish, cover, and refrigerate for 4 to 6 hours.

Cook the game hens: First, remove the hens from the refrigerator about 20 minutes before cooking and season with coarse salt. Preheat the oven to 325°F.

Second, heat the olive oil over medium heat in a large ovenproof skillet, Dutch oven, or braising pan. Brown the seasoned game hens evenly until they are golden, about 3 minutes on each side, for a total of 12 to 15 minutes. Return the browned hens to the ceramic dish.

Third, pour off all but 2 or 3 tablespoons of the olive oil. Add in the garlic cloves and brown them in the oil for 1 to 2 minutes. Increase the heat to high, and deglaze the pan with the white wine. Allow the alcohol to cook off for 2 minutes; return the hens to the pan, and add in the green olives, lemon peel, and oregano sprigs. Pour in the chicken stock, and heat until simmering.

Fourth, cover with a tight-fitting lid. Transfer to the preheated oven and bake until the juices run clear and a meat thermometer registers 160°F when inserted between the leg and the thigh, 35 to 40 minutes.

Fifth, carefully remove the kitchen twine from the hens. Serve laced with the juices and surrounded by the olives, garlic, lemon peel, and oregano sprigs. Squeeze the lemon over the hens just before service.

Note: This savory dish can be readily made substituting the game hens for bone-in and skin-on, split chicken breasts or whole chicken legs. The marinating, cooking methods, and cooking times will be the same.

MINTED CANTALOUPE SORBET

6 Servings ■ ▬ ■ ▬ ■ ▬ ■ ▬ ■ ▬ ■ ▬ ■ ▬ ■ ▬ ■ ▬ ■ ▬ ■

The sandy soil, warm sunny days, and salted ocean breeze of Southern California provide the perfect climate for cantaloupes. As a child I loved to stop by the local roadside stands for sweet melons as well as tomatoes, peppers, and corn. Today, we do the same out on the eastern shore of Maryland. A ripe sweet cantaloupe is hard to beat and makes one of the very best sorbets, a perfect ending to this robust and highly seasoned meal.

1/4 **cup granulated sugar**

3 **tablespoons honey**

1 **cup water**

1/4 **cup fresh chopped mint leaves**

1 **medium cantaloupe**

1 **tablespoon lime juice**

First, combine the sugar, honey, and water in a small saucepan. Bring to a simmer over medium heat, stirring constantly so that the sugar dissolves. Remove the pan from the heat, add in the mint leaves, and steep until the liquid has cooled slightly, about 15 minutes.

Second, wash the outside of the cantaloupe thoroughly. Peel, cut in half, and remove the seeds. Cut into chunks. You should have 4 to 5 cups of melon.

Third, strain and discard the mint leaves. Place the cantaloupe chunks in a stainless mixing bowl. Toss with the lime juice, and pour the warm syrup over the top. Allow the mixture to stand 30 minutes, during which time the melon will be infused with the flavors of honey, lime, and mint.

Third, put the cantaloupe chunks and syrup into a blender fitted with a steel blade and pulse until the mixture is pureed, about 60 seconds.

Fourth, transfer the mixture to an ice cream maker and process according to the manufacturer's instructions. Keep in the freezer until service.

Serve in chilled parfait glasses, and garnish with fresh mint leaves.

Easy Time-Saving and Do-Ahead Tips

SATURDAY:

- *Prepare the gazpacho, cover, and chill.*
- *Marinate the shrimp.*
- *Prepare the sorbet.*

SUNDAY MORNING:

- *Season the game hens and tie their legs together; cover and refrigerate.*

AN HOUR AND A HALF BEFORE DINNER:

- *Remove the game hens from the refrigerator and braise.*
- *Prepare the shrimp.*

Chapter 23

A SABBATH DAY SUPPER

MOLASSES BAKED BEANS

APPLE, BEET, *and* CELERY SALAD

STEAMED BOSTON BROWN BREAD

The political, religious, and cultural life of New England—and the nation—was dramatically shaped by the region's first English settlers, the Puritans. These reformed Protestants came to America to escape religious persecution. They wanted to form churches, villages, and a social order that conformed to the teachings they observed. Their influence over our national ideals—our constitutional principles of democratic and local-based rule, the free exercise of religion, and the separation of church and state—are considerable.

The subsequent decades following their landing at Plymouth Rock saw dozens of independent villages sprout up all along New England's rugged shoreline and inland rivers as the industrious Puritans established a vibrant economy based on farming, fishing, and mills. Hard work and an earnest piety informed all aspects of Puritan life, from their unassuming dress and well-ordered homes to the plain white Congregationalist church buildings, whose tall spires still grace the picturesque New England landscape. Simply prepared and hearty foods were the order of the day.

The New World offered a bounty of unfamiliar foods readily harvested from the vast unspoiled wilderness and rich area waters. The Algonquian Indians gave generously to these people, offering them squash, showing them skills to harvest and prepare corn, and teaching them to tap maple trees for the clear golden syrup.

Beans, especially, became a staple for the Puritans, who adapted the native practice of baking them slowly in earthen pots buried beneath the ground. The Wampanoags seasoned their beans with game, but the Puritans preferred to use the pigs they had imported from home. The culinary result of this cultural blend was a new American classic: pork and beans.

The technique of slow-baking the beans proved especially useful to the Puritans, who took seriously the biblical command to honor the Sabbath by refraining from work. A large pot of beans could be prepared for Saturday supper, then kept warm and eaten both for Sunday breakfast and Sunday dinner, or eaten cold.

This simple meal, though varied in its preparation from state to state and region to region, is still widely enjoyed throughout New England. And while I don't suggest you eat the beans cold on a cold morning, I think you'll agree this hearty dish will more than satisfy a hungry soul.

MOLASSES BAKED BEANS

8 Servings ■ ▪ ▪■ ■ ▪ ▪ ■ ■ ▪ ▪ ■ ▪ ■ ▪ ▪ ■ ▪ ■ ▪ ■ ▪

Those who were fortunate enough to grow up eating delicious, home-baked beans warm from the oven know that there is no comparison. Slow, even cooking is the key to tender, full-flavored baked beans. My grandmother raised her family during hard economic times and looked for nutritious foods that were filling and affordable. She often served her beans with knockwurst Saturday or Sunday and always with Boston brown bread.

2 cups dried great Northern beans

2 quarts cold water, divided

6 ounces salt pork fat or slab bacon

1 bay leaf

6 tablespoons packed dark brown sugar

1 whole clove garlic

1 medium onion, diced

2/3 cup molasses

1/3 cup deli-style mustard

Coarse salt to season

First, wash and pick over the beans; then soak them for 8 hours or overnight.

Second, place the beans into a heavy-bottomed pot with 1 quart of cold water and bring to a boil. Reduce the heat to medium-low and simmer until the beans are tender and the skins begin to break, about 50 minutes.

Oven temperature 250°F.

Third, drain off any excess liquid, leaving only enough to cover the beans by half an inch. Cut the rind from the salt pork fat or slab bacon and slice into 2 or 3 chunks. Add the salt pork fat, bay leaf, brown sugar, garlic, onion, molasses, and mustard to the beans. Transfer to a ceramic casserole or Dutch oven, then cover and bake without stirring until the beans are tender, about 2 1/2 hours. Check the water level from time to time to make sure the beans are covered.

Fourth, when the beans are tender, season with salt (salting too early will make the skins tough) and cook for 30 minutes. Discard the bay leaf before serving.

APPLE, BEET, *and* CELERY SALAD

8 Servings ■ ■■ ■ ■■ ■ ■ ■ ■ ■■ ■ ■ ■■ ■ ■ ■ ■ ■■ ■ ■■■

Parents who think their kids might turn their noses up at beets should give this recipe a try. Beets are high in fiber and essential nutrients. Raw, crunchy beets are delicious and quite different in texture and flavor than cooked beets, especially when paired with crisp apples and crunchy celery.

2 large fresh beets

4 Macintosh apples

4 celery ribs

^{1}/$_4$ cup cider vinegar

^{1}/$_4$ cup granulated sugar

2 tablespoons salad oil

Coarse salt and black pepper

First, cut the tops and bottoms from the beets and cut away the skin with a vegetable peeler.

Second, place the beets on a work surface that has been covered with waxed or parchment paper (to keep from staining the surface). Cut the peeled beets horizontally into 1/4-inch-thick slices. Then cut into matchstick-size strips and transfer to a glass or stainless bowl.

Third, core the apples, cut them into quarters, and slice. Cut away and discard the bottom from the celery ribs, and slice crosswise into bite-size pieces. Chop a little bit of the celery leaves.

Fourth, pour the vinegar into a small mixing bowl and whisk in the sugar until it is dissolved. Whisk in the salad oil, and season the dressing with salt and pepper. Pour the mixture over the beets; add in the apples, celery, and celery leaves; and toss together. Let the salad stand for 10 minutes, re-toss, and serve immediately.

STEAMED BOSTON BROWN BREAD

1 Loaf

Steamed breads were born from necessity long before the advent of modern refrigeration. They stayed moist in their cooking tins and kept well when sealed and stored in a cool root cellar. Many modern Boston brown bread recipes call for replacing the rye flour with all-purpose flour; this works, but the dense texture and nutty flavor are not as good.

For this recipe you'll need an empty 1-pound coffee can (or equal-size can) or a 1-quart steamed-pudding mold in which to steam the bread.

1/2 **cup whole-grain rye flour**

1/2 **cup whole wheat flour**

1/2 **cup cornmeal**

1/2 **teaspoon salt**

1 **cup buttermilk**

1/2 **teaspoon baking soda**

1 **tablespoon hot water**

1/4 **cup dark molasses**

1/2 **cup raisins**

First, whisk the rye flour, whole wheat flour, and cornmeal together with the salt in a mixing bowl. Use a wooden spoon or a mixer fitted with a paddle to slowly incorporate the buttermilk into the dry ingredients. Dissolve the baking soda in the hot water in a separate small bowl and add, along with the molasses, into the dough. Mix on low speed until smooth, about 2 minutes. Fold in the raisins.

Second, butter and flour the 1-pound coffee can or 1-quart mold. Spoon the batter into the can. It should be about 2/3 full. Cover the can tightly with plastic wrap, and then secure the wrap by tying a piece of kitchen twine or a second piece of plastic wrap rolled into a long strand around the top. Cover with aluminum foil to keep the bread from browning. Place the can in a large pot fitted with a round cooling rack or a slotted bottom like you'd have in a pressure cooker, and pour boiling water into the pot until it reaches between 1 and 2 inches up the sides of the can.

Cover the pot with a tight-fitting lid, and simmer over medium heat for 3 hours, adding more water as necessary to maintain the water level.

Third, when the bread is fully steamed, remove the can from the water and cool to room temperature, about 2 hours. Once the bread has cooled, you can serve it warm or keep the loaf sealed in the can. The bread is best served in a day or two.

To remove the bread from the can, turn it over, cut the bottom free with a can opener, and gently but firmly push the loaf out.

Easy Time-Saving and Do-Ahead Tips

SATURDAY:

- *Prepare the brown bread.*
- *Soak the beans.*
- *Prepare the beets and celery; refrigerate in sealed containers.*

Chapter 24

SOUTHERN TRADITIONS

GLAZED COUNTRY-BAKED HAM

GINGER-PEACH CHUTNEY

THYME-SCENTED SCALLOPED POTATOES

SALLY LUNN BREAD

BAKED SPAGHETTI SQUASH

PINEAPPLE MANGO UPSIDE-DOWN CAKE

Baked ham has long been a Sunday dinner favorite. In the Southeast, especially, where traditions run deep and where roots are buried firmly in the soil of our early American colonies, a baked-ham dinner is standard Sunday fare. Different varieties of American hams, each with its own distinct flavor and style, were created throughout these developing lands—from Virginia, home of the famous Smithfield hams, down to the Carolinas and Georgia, and over the mountains to Kentucky and Tennessee.

Smoking as a way to preserve meats is an ancient practice. In America on family farms and plantations, and in local communities, it became an art form. During the fall after the fattened hogs were slaughtered, the cured, whole bone-in legs were then sewn into muslin bags and hung in smokehouses to pick up the smoke's rich flavor and develop a deep terracotta color. Each region created a distinct flavor by using a variety of methods for feeding, curing, and smoking. Feeding hogs on corn, peanuts, or even peaches; brine-curing the meat and rubbing it with various spices, salt, and sugar; and finally smoking the joints over the choicest woods gave each farmer's meaty and succulent creation a signature aroma and taste. A great ham was cured for months and became a long-anticipated treat, along with the garden's first offerings for springtime dinners—especially on Easter Sunday.

Thomas Jefferson, America's third president and one of the authors of the Declaration of Independence, was also famous for his fine hams, his gardens, and his hospitality. He grew more than 250 kinds of vegetables at his Virginia home, Monticello, including a great variety of squash, beans, and peas. His table was often filled with the good company of friends and family. The hours spent attending to his farm and enjoying his loved ones and guests were among his happiest. Shouldn't that be true for us all?

The tradition of an open door is not simply a sign of Southern hospitality, of course, but is a quintessentially American habit. When we open our homes, we open our hearts. And when we offer our best and welcome our guests to the bounty of our table, we continue this fine tradition, a tradition well worth keeping.

Surely the best Sunday dinners are those where everyone becomes part of the family. We all have our favorite expressions of hospitality and our favorite meals. Few could be a more appropriate expression than to offer our family and friends such a time-honored meal as this one.

GLAZED COUNTRY-BAKED HAM

12 Servings

Most hams today are water-added, and while they can be used for making this delicious ham dinner, taking the time to find a hand-cured, bone-in, fully cooked ham with natural juices is well worth the effort. Not only does the ham have a better natural flavor, it will also be less processed. The ham bone can later be used to make a delicious meal, such as split pea soup or baked beans.

BAKED HAM

1 (10-pound) sugar-cured smoked ham

GLAZE

1/4 teaspoon ground cinnamon

1/4 teaspoon ground cloves

2 tablespoons deli-style mustard

1/2 cup packed dark brown sugar

Oven temperature 325°F.

Make the ham: First, rinse the ham under cool running water and dry it thoroughly with paper towels. Use a sharp knife to carefully trim away the outer skin from the ham, leaving a layer of fat and a collar of skin around the shank bone. You may trim away some of the fat, as well, but leave a 1/2-inch layer. Score the fat on the top of the ham in a 1- to 2-inch diamond pattern, cutting just slightly into the meat.

Second, place the ham in a shallow roasting pan. Place the pan on the lower oven rack and bake until the ham reaches an internal temperature of 140°F, about 1 hour and 45 minutes.

Prepare the glaze: Thoroughly combine the cinnamon, cloves, mustard, and brown sugar in a small mixing bowl. When the ham has baked for the prescribed amount of time, brush the top and sides evenly with the glaze. Increase the oven temperature to 350°F and continue baking until the glaze is bubbly, about 20 to 30 additional minutes.

GINGER-PEACH CHUTNEY

12 Servings

Though generally associated with Indian cuisine, chutney is actually English in origin and was one of the best ways to preserve exotic fruits during colonial times. This wonderful, tangy gingery chutney is a perfect complement to the smoky ham. It is also excellent when nectarines, apricots, or plums are substituted for the peaches.

1/4 **cup packed dark brown sugar**

2 **tablespoons cider vinegar**

I **cup peach juice or nectar**

I **cup peach preserves**

4 **cups fresh sliced peaches or frozen sliced peaches, thawed**

I **tablespoon fresh minced ginger**

I **small red chili pepper, seeded and minced**

I **cinnamon stick**

First, combine the brown sugar, vinegar, peach juice or nectar, and preserves in a heavy-bottomed saucepan. Bring to a boil over medium-high heat, and add the peach slices, ginger, chili pepper, and cinnamon stick. Lower the heat to medium and simmer, stirring frequently, until the peaches are fully cooked and the liquid is thick and bubbling, 30 to 40 minutes.

Second, remove the pan from the stove and cool to room temperature. Remove and discard the cinnamon stick. Spoon the chutney into a stainless or glass bowl. Cover and refrigerate for at least 2 hours and up to 3 days before serving.

THYME-SCENTED SCALLOPED POTATOES

12 Servings

One can hardly think of ham without thinking of scalloped potatoes—the two are simply made for each other—and these potatoes are truly exceptional. Using sharp cheddar cheese at the end adds extra zing to this creamy casserole.

10 medium potatoes, peeled and cut into 1/4-inch slices

1 medium onion, thinly sliced

1 tablespoon fresh chopped thyme

1/2 cup (1 stick) butter

2 cups whole milk, as needed

1 1/2 teaspoons salt

1/2 teaspoon white pepper

1/2 cup grated sharp cheddar cheese

Preheat the oven to 325°F.

First, butter the bottom and sides of a 13 x 9-inch baking dish. Arrange a layer of the potato on the bottom of the dish, then sprinkle with onion slices and a little thyme. Dot with butter and repeat. Finish with a final layer of potatoes dotted with butter.

Third, whisk the milk with the salt and white pepper. Slowly pour the mixture over the potatoes to fill the casserole a little more than halfway. (The potatoes will cook down as they are baked.)

Fourth, cover the dish tightly with nonstick foil or foil that has been sprayed with oil. Place the baking dish on a baking sheet and transfer to the oven. Bake until the potatoes are tender when tested with the tip of a knife, about 1 1/2 hours.

Fifth, remove the foil. Increase the oven temperature to 350°F. Sprinkle with the grated cheese and bake until the top is browned and the casserole is bubbling, about 30 more minutes.

SALLY LUNN BREAD

1 Bundt Loaf ■ ■ ■ ■ ■ ■ ■ ■ ■ ■ ■ ■ ■ ■ ■ ■ ■ ■ ■

This creamy-textured bread, popular in the Southern colonies and traditionally baked in a fluted tube or Bundt pan, makes a beautiful centerpiece. Legend has it that Sally Lunn was a young girl from eighteenth-century Bath, England, who cried sweet tears into the bread that bears her name. Most likely the name came from the Italian bakers who pushed their carts through the street of this once-fashionable British spa, crying "Sole luna!" ("Sun and moon") to describe the bread's golden crust and soft, creamy center.

1 package (1 1/2 teaspoons) active dry yeast

1/4 cup warm whole milk, about 110°F

1 cup whole milk

1/4 cup granulated sugar

1/2 cup (1 stick) unsalted butter

1/2 cup shortening

3 cups all-purpose flour, divided

3 large eggs, room temperature, lightly beaten

1 cup cake flour

1 teaspoon salt

Oven temperature 350°F.

First, sprinkle the yeast over the 1/4 cup warm milk and let stand for 1 minute; then stir until the yeast is dissolved.

Second, scald 1 cup of milk with the sugar by heating it in a small saucepan just to the point of boiling. Remove it from heat, add in the butter and shortening, and swirl until they are melted. Cool in the pan until lukewarm.

Third, combine the dissolved yeast with the lukewarm milk in the bowl of a mixer fitted with a paddle. Turn the mixer on low speed and gradually add in 2 cups of the all-purpose flour, 1/2 cup at a time, until the flour is fully incorporated. Continue mixing until the batter is smooth and elastic, about 2 minutes. Scrape down the sides of the bowl with a rubber spatula.

Fourth, turn the mixer to low speed and gradually add in the 3 lightly beaten eggs until they are fully incorporated. Then add in the remaining 1 cup of all-purpose flour, 1/4 cup at a time; continue to beat on low speed until the dough is once again smooth, about 2 more minutes.

Fifth, whisk the cake flour together with the salt in a separate bowl. Turn the mixer to low speed, and slowly add the mixture into the dough, 1/4 cup at a time. Scrape down the sides of the bowl with a rubber spatula. Replace the paddle with a dough hook, and knead on low speed for 5 minutes. The dough will now have a buttery-smooth, silky texture. It will be much softer than traditional bread dough. Cover the dough with a clean tea towel and set in a draft-free place until it has doubled in volume, about 1 1/2 hours.

Sixth, lightly butter a 10-inch Bundt pan. Beat the raised dough down with a spatula or wooden spoon and turn evenly into the buttered pan. Cover with a clean tea towel and let rise until the dough has doubled in volume by half, about 40 minutes.

Seventh, brush the top of the dough with a little milk and bake for 50 to 60 minutes. As it bakes, the bread will rise above the rim of the pan.

Eighth, when the bread is done baking, it will have a deep golden hue on the outside and a dense, soft feel to it when squeezed gently. Cool in the pan for 5 minutes, and then turn the loaf onto a baking rack to cool.

BAKED SPAGHETTI SQUASH

12 Servings

Spaghetti squash has gained popularity only recently, though it has been around for over five thousand years. English colonists called it vegetable squash because its unique crunch and tender texture resembles a vegetable more than other squash varieties do. Because of its hard shell, it is mostly thought of as a winter squash, so named because they keep well into the winter months. Many people think, however, that the spaghetti squash is really the origin of the canary-yellow summer squash.

1 large spaghetti squash
2 tablespoons butter
Salt and pepper to taste

Oven temperature 325°F.

First, cut the squash in half lengthwise and scoop the seeds from the center. Rub the center of each half with a tablespoon of butter and season with salt and pepper. Place the squash directly onto the top rack of the oven or on a baking sheet and bake until the strands are translucent but still crunchy, 50 to 60 minutes. You can bake this alongside the potatoes and ham dishes.

Second, remove the squash from the oven and transfer to wire racks until they are cool enough to handle, about 10 minutes. Scrape the flesh from the shells with a fork, twisting a little as you do to separate the yellow strands. Transfer immediately to a wide serving bowl and serve with additional butter, or cool and then reheat in the microwave in a covered casserole.

PINEAPPLE MANGO UPSIDE-DOWN CAKE

12 servings ▪▪▪▪▪▪▪▪▪▪▪▪▪▪▪▪▪▪▪▪▪▪▪▪▪▪▪▪▪

Fruit upside-down cakes have been around for ages—especially those made with pineapples, which were a symbol of hospitality throughout colonial America. There was a time when not everyone had an oven and cakes were baked in skillets set off to the side of an open hearth. The fruit on the bottom protected the cake from burning and gave it needed moisture.

You can substitute two 14-ounce cans of whole pineapple rings in syrup for the fresh pineapple. If you do, skip the "prepare the pineapple" steps in the recipe.

FRUIT

3/4 cup granulated sugar

1 cup water

1 medium fresh pineapple, peeled, cored, and cut into 1/2-inch rings

2 cups mango chunks

CAKE

2 1/4 cups cake flour

2 1/2 teaspoons baking powder

1/2 teaspoon salt

2/3 cup unsalted butter

1 cup granulated sugar

3 large eggs, room temperature

1 1/2 teaspoons pure vanilla extract

1/2 cup whole milk

1/2 cup reserved pineapple syrup

TOPPING

3 tablespoons unsalted butter

1/2 cup packed light brown sugar

1/4 cup reserved pineapple syrup

Add the sugar and water to a large saucepan and whisk until the sugar is dissolved. Bring the liquid to a boil over medium heat and simmer for 5 minutes. Place the pineapple rings into the sugar syrup in 2 separate batches, turning once and simmering each batch for 3 to 4 minutes. Transfer the slices from the syrup into a glass dish and let the pineapple rings cool to room temperature. When you are done simmering the pineapple, remove the pan from the heat and add the fresh mango chunks to the pineapple syrup. Cool to room temperature, then drain the mango chunks and reserve the syrup. (You should have about 3/4 cup reserved syrup.)

Oven temperature 350°F.

Make the cake batter: First, sift together the cake flour, baking powder, and salt in a medium bowl. Set aside.

Second, use a mixer fitted with a paddle to cream the butter with the sugar until light and fluffy, 6 to 8 minutes. Scrape down the sides of the bowl with a rubber spatula. Turn the speed to medium, and add the eggs one at a time, mixing well after each addition. Add the vanilla.

Third, reduce the mixer speed to low and add in the dry ingredients and the milk alternately in 3 stages. Mix long enough to form a smooth batter. Increase the mixer speed to medium, and pour in 1/2 cup of the reserved pineapple syrup. Beat for 1 minute.

Make the topping: Melt the butter over medium heat in a 10-inch round ovenproof skillet with 2 1/4-inch sides. Remove the skillet from the heat, sprinkle the brown sugar evenly over the bottom, and pour in the remaining 1/4 cup reserved pineapple syrup.

Assemble the cake: Crowd the pineapple slices into the bottom of the skillet and cut any remaining slices to fit around the edges and up the sides of the skillet. Place a chunk of mango in the center of each pineapple ring and in any spaces between the rings. Slowly spread the cake batter over the fruit.

Place the cake onto the middle oven rack. Bake 40 to 45 minutes until a wooden pick comes out clean when inserted in the middle. Cool on a wire rack for 5 minutes before inverting onto your favorite serving plate. Serve slices topped with freshly whipped cream.

Easy Time-Saving and Do-Ahead Tips

SATURDAY:

- *Prepare the chutney.*
- *Bake the pineapple cake.*
- *Bake the bread.*

SUNDAY MORNING:

- *Trim and score the ham.*
- *Prepare the glaze.*
- *Peel the potatoes and cover with cold water.*

TWO HOURS BEFORE DINNER:

- *Bake the ham and the potatoes.*

Coming Home

Coming home. The words warm our hearts with memories and with anticipation.

It has been a constant thread—through good times and bad—and is still very much a part of our family life. As our family has grown, this tradition has continued, and we have been blessed to be guests in their homes for everyday memories and special celebrations. And no matter what twists and turns life brings, there will always be a place at our Sunday table and a hearty welcome home—for our children, their children, and our friends. The Sunday table is like that—it is a weekly homecoming, a time and place of memories where everyone in the family knows they will be welcomed with open arms—a place of acceptance, a place where unconditional love is spoken, a place where memories are made.

When I was growing up, Grandma's Sunday dinner table was where the whole family gathered when an announcement was to be made, when a baby had been born, or when one of my uncles had bought a new automobile. (Our family albums are filled with pictures of kids and cars!) It was the place to remember birthdays, too. Once a month the whole clan would gather to celebrate all of the birthdays that fell in that particular month. Special occasions—a graduation, a baptism, a new house—were recognized as a family. Like the bright pieces that form a mosaic, those singular moments created memories that will last a lifetime.

Not all of us have large families living nearby. Some have parents who have passed on. Others have let many years go by since they last came together. But Sunday celebrations can still be a time for opening our hearts and our table to those who are family by choice as well as by birth.

The Sunday dinner table is the ideal place to build extended family. Church friends, neighbors, coworkers, childhood pals, and college classmates who are invited for Sunday dinner often become cherished friends with whom we take vacations and celebrate special occasions. These are the friendships that endure through challenge and triumph. And Sunday dinner is where it all begins, nurturing an investment far beyond any earthly value, creating a world we are glad to come home to.

There was always extra room at my grandmother's and my mother's tables, and my wife and I wanted to recreate that sense of openness in our home. From the time they were very small, each of our children knew that their friends were welcome to join us. Sunday dinner became the natural place to bring new acquaintances and an easy way for them to introduce the special people in their lives.

Even after our children ventured off to college, using their weekends home to run around and see their friends, we knew they'd be at our house for Sunday dinner. When they brought friends with them, they usually phoned ahead—but not always. There were a few times when our kids would simply show up and expect a warm family welcome for whomever they brought with them. And though we occasionally needed to run to the market or creatively raid the refrigerator, we still managed to make room at the Sunday table.

Our children are now grown and have embarked on lives of their own. Our family of five has grown to eight and now includes grandchildren. Like my grandparents, we are always ready to expand our table and our open invitation to Sunday dinner.

So join us, if you will. Set the table with your Sunday best, prepare the feast with loving hands, and open your hearts and front doors wide. The family is coming home!

Index